The Physical Conditions of the
Elizabethan Public
Playhouse

LONDON : HUMPHREY MILFORD

OXFORD UNIVERSITY PRESS

The Physical Conditions of the Elizabethan Public Playhouse

BY

WILLIAM J. LAWRENCE

Cambridge

HARVARD UNIVERSITY PRESS

1927

PRINTED AT THE HARVARD UNIVERSITY PRESS
CAMBRIDGE, MASS., U.S.A.

To

WILLIAM POEL

PREFACE

37499

THIS book is a fusion of several lectures forming part of an undergraduate course, which I had the honour of giving, by gracious invitation, at Harvard University and repeating at Radcliffe College in the first half of the academic year of 1925–26. With the view of rendering the whole more serviceable to students, the matter has been recast, and some supplementary details appended in footnotes. The book represents my maturer conclusions on a complex subject which has held me in willing bondage, despite the occasional obtrusion of other interests, for more than a quarter of a century. Not that I am foolish enough to claim that mere length of service entitles me to pose as Sir Oracle; so multifarious are the ramifications and intricacies of my theme that it must be reckoned in the category of those vexed questions on which one never says the last word, only the last word but one. I recall how, some years ago, when the late Professor Thornton Shirley Graves and I were engaged on a private controversy on certain moot Elizabethan points, — we were at a safe distance, the Atlantic being between us, — he once concluded a subtle argument with the avowal, "Such is my firm conviction to-day — but I won't guarantee that it will be my opinion twelve months hence." Therein spoke the authentic voice of the investigating spirit: at all hazards, one must cherish the open mind. Be the shortcomings of my book, however, what they may, I am hopeful that it will prove an inspiring object-lesson to future labourers in the field and incite them to make steady and resolute endeavour to increase the sum-total of our knowledge of the Elizabethan theatre. Unfortunately, there is little prospect of new documentary evidence coming to light, but I feel confident that inductive reasoning, allied with profound scholarship, can still achieve something material.

I desire to express my acknowledgments to Lieutenant-Colonel Charles Archer, the brother and executor of my sometime colleague, William Archer, for his kindness in giving me the use of some of his brother's unpublished studies, from which serviceable quotation has been made. I am likewise duly grateful to the Clarendon Press for permitting me to copy the very clear reproduction of the Swan drawing made in *Shakespeare's England*.

W. J. L.

Monkstown, Co. Dublin
March, 1927

*The Physical Conditions of the
Elizabethan Public
Playhouse*

provide accommodation on the sides for the stool-holding gallants, and could not invariably have confined their action to the back. One is confirmed in this opinion on finding that the stage of the first Fortune theatre was 43 feet broad by 27½ feet deep.[1] As the Fortune was modelled, in all but its shape, on the Globe, we have here a fairly sound indication of the normal type.

There are other debatable points. If you look at the Dutch sketch of the Swan, made in 1596, you will see that De Witt depicts its stage as un-enclosed on the three sides and borne up by trestles. That, I think, was a very primitive sort of arrangement, and was followed only where the stage had to be in whole or part removable. The Fortune contract bearing witness, we know that by the close of the sixteenth century the sides of the stage had begun to be paled in. Without this paling there could have been no excavation beneath the stage; yet excavation to provide depth enough for trap-work was essential, otherwise the stage would have had to be built immoderately high. Unfortunately we have no clear evidence as to the normal height of the stage, but it can be safely approximated. My belief is that the average public-theatre stage could

[1] William Archer on "The Fortune Theatre, 1600" in *Shakespeare Jahrbuch*, 1908, pp. 159 ff. For the full text of the Fortune contract, see Chambers, *The Elizabethan Stage*, ii, 436. Illustrations of a scale model of the Fortune are given in *The Architectural Review*, vol. xxxi, 54-5.

have been little over five feet high, else there would have been no reason to fear incursion from the occupants of the yard. That there was a risk of this order is shown by the circumstance that all the theatres, from the first Globe onwards, had an ornamental balustrade protecting the stage on its three sides. It would seem that, in time of severe rain, the drenched groundlings were greatly tempted to climb somewhere into shelter — the reason why, besides the provision of the stage balustrade, a fencing of iron pikes was placed in front of the gentlemen's rooms, or ground stand, which circulated round about two thirds of the yard.[1]

The fact that no trace is to be found of the stage balustrade in De Witt's sketch of the Swan is still

[1] Note that the Fortune contract specifies that the stage is to be "paled in belowe with good stronge and sufficient newe oken bourdes, and likewise the lower story of the said frame withinside, and the same lower storie to be alsoe laid over and fenced with strong yron pykes." Strange to say, none of the many conjectural reconstructions of the Elizabethan public theatre shows these iron pikes bristling around the yard. Nor are they to be remarked in De Witt's sketch of the Swan. In A. Forestier's sectional plan for the Fortune, reproduced in *The Illustrated London News* for August 12, 1911, the stage rails are shown, as likewise a railing a little in front of the stage, to keep back the groundlings. There is no warrant for this ground railing, which, in the circumstance, is superfluous. It was probably due to a misconception of the Fortune contract.

Relative to the iron spikes round the lower part of the auditorium, it is noteworthy that in the picture-stage era they were transferred to the front of the orchestra. The orchestra spikes are plainly to be seen in some of Hogarth's minor sketches.

another proof of the primitiveness of the Swan stage. That the balustrade was *in situ* in the first Globe is shown by an allusion in *The Black Book*, by T. M., published in 1604.[1] After making his appearance from below, Lucifer delivers a prologue in which he says:

> And now that I have vaulted up so high,
> Above the stage rails of this earthen globe,
> I must turn actor and join companies,
> To share my comic sleek-ey'd villanies.

Although, as I have indicated, the primitive theatre stage was devoid of these rails, the curious point is that the temporary stages erected from time to time in the college halls of Cambridge were regularly furnished with them for years before the first London theatre was built. In the accounts of Trinity College for the year 1562–63 one finds the item: "It' to Rycharde Bell ij dais et dim' setting vpp the stage & Raile at *Christus Triumphans*, ij^s. vj^d." [2]

Later entries in the accounts of the same college show that the custom of providing stage rails there when plays were given persisted until after the Restoration. In the accounts for 1614–15, we have:

Item to James Manutij for paynting the stage, vj^{li}. vij^s. vj^d.
Item for paynting the Rayles on the stage ij^s. vj^d.[3]

---

[1] Reprinted in Bullen's *Middleton*, viii, 8. It is not certain that Middleton was the author.

[2] Malone Society *Collections*, ii, 2, p. 163.   [3] *Ibid.*, p. 172.

So, too, in the Carpenter's bill for 1662–63, we get, under date January 13, an item of "31 foote of railes about ye Stage, 5. 7." [1] And another entry shows that John Piers was paid £3. 9. 1. for miscellaneous services, including "painting ye Railes."

On the point of court usage we have no clear evidence before the Caroline period, but it is certain that at that period the court stage had rails. Why these should have been provided, it is difficult to say; it cannot be pretended that the court gallants occasionally emulated the groundlings and ran amok. Inigo Jones's interesting design for the proscenium arch and tent scene in Habington's *The Queen of Arragon*, a play originally produced at Whitehall in 1640, has recently been reproduced; [2] and in it is clearly to be detected a low balustrade running on a line with the frontispiece.

There is good reason to believe that, from 1599 for at least three quarters of a century, all the London theatres, public or private (which means popular or select), had this balustrade. True, it is not shown in the well-known view of the Red Bull

[1] Malone Society *Collections*, ii, 2, pp. 175, 176.

[2] See Allardyce Nicoll, *British Drama*, p. 106. Note that it was in the meridian of the first Charles's reign that court plays (and court plays and some university plays only) first came to be provided with movable scenery. The rails in the design in Nicoll should be compared with the rails in the design for the Royal Cockpit theatre at Whitehall, reproduced by J. Q. Adams, *Shakespearean Playhouses*, p. 396. At the Royal Cockpit, the rails were 18 inches high.

ROXANA
TRAGÆDIA

A plagiarij
vnguibus
vindicata
aucta, et
agnita ab
authore
Gulielmo
Alabastro.

stage, but it must be borne in mind that the view depicts the old theatre as it was in Commonwealth days, after it had been dismantled by the Puritans, and at a time when performances were surreptitious. On the other hand, two other views of early seventeenth-century stages — the one given on the title-page of the Latin play of *Roxana* in 1632, and the other on the title-page of Richards's tragedy of *Messalina* in 1640 — both present the balustrade. Note that the *Roxana* engraving shows rows of balusters with a connective top rail, the normal system in the playhouses.[1]

If proof were demanded of me of my statement that the stage depicted in Kirkman's view of the Red Bull is not in its pristine state, I should hasten to advance it from Smith's play, *The Hector of Germanie*, which was printed in 1615 with the intimation that it had been acted "by young men of the city at the Red Bull and Curtain." The text is undivided, but toward the close of the play, the two fools, an Englishman and a Frenchman, come on at the French court and pretend that the characters on the stage are assembled there to act a drama. The Englishman says to them, "Begin, begin, we are set"; and an accompanying direction or marginal note tells the actor to "sit on the Railes."

[1] Reproduced in *Shakespeare's England*, ii, 286. Enlargements of both views are given by Nicoll, *British Drama*, p. 70.

A reference in the fifth stanza of the topical ballad-epilogue to Davenant's comedy, *The Man's the Master*,[1] sung at the Duke's Theatre in 1668, shows that, much as the Restoration stage differed from the earlier stage, it was still maintaining the balustrade. Exactly when it disappeared, one cannot say, but it is not to be traced at any later period.

Elsewhere I have dealt exhaustively with the intricate problem of early stage traps, and must content myself now by giving a bald summary of my conclusions. Before 1600 only two traps were employed, one of no particular intricacy; but less than a score of years later no fewer than five were in regular use. Progressiveness of this order shows the futility of endeavoring to picture a typical Elizabethan theatre. To generalize is only to distort the historical perspective, because, side by side with the tendency toward standardization, there was growth.

At the back of the old platform-stage stood an oddly fronted house, consisting of a ground floor and two stories, surmounted by a garret which rose above the theatre-building and is clearly to be seen in the old map-views of the Bankside theatres.[2] This house was commonly known as "the tiring-house," because it was in one of its upper rooms that the players attired themselves; but it also answered as

---

[1] Cited by Robert W. Lowe, *Thomas Betterton*, pp. 40, 41.
[2] See views in Allardyce Nicoll, *British Drama*, pp. 66 and 68.

THE
TRAGEDY
of
MESSALLINA
by
N. RICHARDS.

London printed
for
Dan: Frere.
1640

MESSALLINA

SILIVS

a property store, besides affording accommodation for the musicians and a few spectators. Between the tiring-house and the auditorium proper there was, architecturally speaking, unity in disparity. The three floors of the tiring-house were on the same level with the lowermost parts of the three surrounding galleries, though there was a perceptible break on either side of the stage.

Just a word or two, before I proceed to make minute examination of the tiring-house, about these three galleries. From one source or another one is apt to get the erroneous impression that they were of a vast height. To some extent, Jusserand voices popular opinion when he writes of the Bankside playhouses as "huge polygonal towers." [1] Polygonal may pass, but huge towers they certainly were not. But it is not difficult to see how this idea arose in M. Jusserand's mind and in the minds of those who agree with him on the point. Distorting the truth for a special purpose, one or two of the old map-views of South London do represent the Bankside theatres as buildings of a great altitude and of a greater height than breadth. [2] But a

---

[1] J. J. Jusserand, *A Literary History of the English People* (2d edit. 1926), ii, 307.

[2] Particularly in Visscher's map of 1616 (see A. H. Thorndike, *Shakespeare's Theatre*, frontispiece). The true proportions of the old theatres and amphitheatres are best indicated in Hondius's map of 1611 (Thorndike, *ibid.*, p. 33), and in Hollar's map of 1647 (for reproductions, see Ordish's *Early London Theatres*, p. 239, and J. Q. Adams's *Shakespearean Playhouses*, p. 260).

moment's thought will show why this was done. Maps were mostly bought by visitors to the city, and the theatres were places of prime resort whose location it was desirable readily to determine. Hence the magnifying of the buildings on the maps as well as the occasional inscription of their names. What we require to grasp is that the Elizabethan public theatre, like the bull- and bear-baiting amphi-theatres,[1] had considerably more width than height. Although differing in shape, the first Fortune was modelled on the Globe, and for this reason the measurements given in the Fortune contract are highly instructive. The three galleries were re-spectively 12, 11, and 9 feet high, or a total of 32 feet. Add about 9 feet for the tiring-house garret, and you get a total height of 41 feet. As the theatre was 80 feet square, it is obvious that the building was twice as broad as it was tall.[2] So, pray, let us hear no more of "huge polygonal towers."

I return now to the tiring-house. Its most im-portant office was the utility of its curiously com-posite façade as a permanent, though highly adap-tive, background for the play. In presenting doors and windows and a balcony in their normal places, this façade bore some resemblance to an ordinary house-front; but the similitude was dissipated by the

[1] See the section from Aggas's map of 1560, given in Ordish, *Early London Theatres*, p. 126.

[2] William Archer on "The Fortune Theatre, 1600," in *Shakespeare Jahrbuch*, 1908, p. 161.

two sets of curtains, one above the other, with which
it was embellished. Let us begin by considering the
characteristics of its ground floor, the floor which
stood on stage level. In the centre was a curtained
space of the proportions of an average-sized room,
and a little removed from this on either side was a
substantial door. These two doors formed the normal way of entrance and departure adopted by the
players. There was a third possible entrance, but
consideration of this may conveniently be post-
poned until later. The only early theatre view that
gives us a sight of the two normal entering doors is
De Witt's sketch of the Swan, and in this the doors
are of a massive bivalved order with immense hinges.
Whether this arrangement applied to all the Elizabethan houses or was peculiar to the Swan no evidence exists to show. But the doors had other
utilities besides serving as entrance ways and had
to be fitted up accordingly. Often they formed a
prime feature of the background of the action, now
serving as exterior doors and now as room doors.
For this reason they had to be provided with locks,
bolts and ring-knockers. This plain fact negatives
the supposition — which has occasionally been
given expression to,[1] and was actually taken as
scientifically accurate by Mr. W. Noel Hills when
designing his map of "the Shakespearean Stage,"

[1] Cf. John Corbin on "Shakspere his own Stage Manager," in
the *Century Magazine* for December, 1911, pp. 263, 264.

— that what in stage directions were so often called doors were seldom anything more than curtained entrances. On this point, we must not allow ourselves to be deceived, as others have been before us, by the evidence of Kirkman's Red Bull print, which, as I have said, represents that house in the Commonwealth period, after it had been dismantled by the Puritans, and when acting could be given only surreptitiously on a hastily rigged-up stage.

Nor is this the only untenable theory that has been advanced concerning the doors and their usages. One recalls Brodmeier's rash assumption [1] that, when one door was supposed to be the door of a given house, the other door had also necessarily to belong to that house. In some unpublished notes on the Elizabethan stage by my former collaborator, the late William Archer, which came into my possession after his death, I find him writing on this point:

On the stage of the Swan drawing there might indeed be some difficulty in getting an audience to accept "the one house, one door" principle; but, if the rear-stage opening interposed between the two doors (as it must have done in the majority of theatres), and still more if the doors were oblique, there could be no difficulty whatever.

Brodmeier's fundamental weakness is that he makes all his deductions exclusively from De Witt's sketch and ignores rebutting evidence: an attitude

[1] *Die Shakespeare-Bühne nach den alten Bühnenweisungen.* See also William Archer's review of this book in *The Quarterly Review*, No. 415, 1908, pp. 448 ff.

which compelled him to postulate curtains between
the pillars of the "shadow" — a plausible theory
which for long led several conscientious investigators astray. On the subject of oblique doors I shall
have something to say later. We have first to consider the evidence proving that the doors had knock-
ers, bolts, and locks. Some of the evidence is,
strictly speaking, only private-theatre evidence, but
it seems to me that on the score of the fitting-up
of doors, there is no great likelihood of any serious difference between public-theatre and private-
theatre practice. Middleton's comedy, *The Phoenix*
yields proof that the playhouse of Paul's, the scene
of its production, had ring-knockers on the doors.
There is a situation at the beginning of the fourth
act where one of the characters accidentally jars
the ring, and, all unconsciously, gives the sign to
the maid for the opening of the door. Afterward,
in the third scene of the act, the right person gives
the sign. Heywood's *The English Traveller* is evidence for the Cockpit at a later period. In act II,
scene 2, the action passes before Old Lionel's house.
A direction says: "Exeunt all except Reignald who
locks the door"; and Reignald presently "retires."
Then Old Lionel comes on and "knocks loudly."
Reignald comes forward, and asks, "Said you, sir
— did your hand touch that hammer?"

Evidence of the bolting of doors is not very
abundant, but we have an example in *The Twins* of

W. Rider, a Salisbury Court tragedy of the Caroline period, first published in 1655. At the opening of the fifth act one finds the direction, "Enter Charmia in her night gown, with a prayer book and a taper, boults the door and sits down." As the door here bolted was not one of the two normal entering doors, I am constrained before proceeding to discuss the locking of doors, to deal minutely with the third mode of entrance. Usually, when two or more characters enter separately, the formula is "Enter A at the one door, B at the other door," though for "the other door" we occasionally get "another door." [1] Of the more explicit instruction, examples abound in Massinger; see *The Bondman*, v, 3; *The Renegado*, v, 3, and *The City Madam*, iv, 1, and v, 3. But besides this common formula, and its variant, we get occasional reference to a middle or farther door, a door to whose existence no old theatre view testifies and whose exact position we have to determine. The description at times of this entrance as a "farther door," shows that, although intermediate, it was not on a level with the two normal doors, and must therefore have stood in a recess. That being so, there was no other place for it save at the back of the rear stage, or inner room, otherwise the curtained space between the two com-

---

[1] For some Shakespearean examples, see *Shakespeare's England*, ii, 304, note. Shakespeare also employs the expression "at several doors," meaning practically the same thing.

monly-used doors. Let us consider some examples. In *The Second Maiden's Tragedy*, a Globe play of Shakespeare's later time, we have in act IV, scene 3, "Enter the Tyrant agen at a farder dore, which opened, bringes hym to the tombe, wher the Lady lies buried. The tomb here discovered, ritchly set forthe." This is clumsily put, and, if written by the author, dubs him amateur. What happened was that the curtains of the rear stage drew and revealed the tomb, after which the Tyrant (who had previously gone off by one of the regular doors) reëntered through the door at the back. This explains the direction in act V, scene 1, "Enter Votarius to the door within," the word "within" indicating the rear stage. I am not disposed to offer any opinion as to the authorship of this play beyond what I have said about the long stage direction; but it is curious that Swinburne should have been imbued with the belief that Middleton wrote it, seeing that in one of Middleton's acknowledged plays *Your Five Gallants*, written *circa* 1607, or about a lustrum before *The Second Maiden's Tragedy*, we get, in act I, scene 2, "Enter Goldstone, Pursenet, Tailby, Frippery, Primero and Boy at the farther door." A textual reference to this door as a "back door" occurs in *A Wife for A Month*, II, 6, the scene preceding the masque, where the Second Servant, referring to the women who are crushing to get in to see the entertainment, says:

Look to that back door,
And keep it fast; they swarm like flies about it.

Presently, through that door, the Citizens' wives troop in to enjoy the masque.

The use of the middle door is practically always implied where we get the instruction, "Enter behind." This was the common mode of entrance for eavesdroppers, though in cases where the rear-stage curtains happened to be closed, their actual entry was not seen, and they simply peeped through the curtains. The remoteness of the door explains the folio direction in *Hamlet*, v, 1, l. 60, "Enter Hamlet and Horatio a farre off." It is noteworthy that some sixty lines are then spoken before Hamlet addresses the gravedigger.[1]

We have seen that the third way of entrance was farther back than the other two, and it remains now to prove that it was situated between them. That is a task of no great difficulty. Thus, in William Percy's *The Faery Pastorall*, written *circa* 1600, we get the direction, at a juncture where three characters come on simultaneously, "They entrd at severall doores, Learchus at the Midde doore." So, too, in the opening direction in *Eastward Hoe*, a

[1] Creizenach (*The English Stage in the Time of Shakespeare*, p. 373) places the middle door, not at the back of the recess, but immediately behind the curtains. This is surely a mistake. Unless we can conceive of the door as a temporary expedient, a sort of stage property to be placed in position when required, its station here would have obscured the rear-stage action.

Blackfriars play of 1605, reference is made to "the middle door." Again, in a much later play, Burnell's tragedy of *Langartha*, acted at the Werburgh Street Theatre, Dublin, in 1640, we get the direction in the second act, "Enter Inguar in the middle." Armed with these clues, we are in a position to realize the situation at the end of *The Travailes of the Three English Brothers*, a Curtain play of 1607, where, after Fame has divided the stage into three parts, a direction says, "Enter three severall waies the three Brothers." Other situations in other plays are elucidated by this argument and help to substantiate it. Look, for example, at the stage business indicated in Jonson's *The Silent Woman*, v, 3, where Truewit, just as he is about to send for Morose, says: "Come, Dauphine, . . . thou shalt keepe one dore and I another, and then Clerimont in the midst, that he may have no means of escape from their cavalling, when they grow hot at once."

Resort to the use of the middle door also explains the puzzling action indicated in a vague stage direction in *A Woman is a Weathercock*, III, 2, running: "Scudmore passes [through] one door, and enters at the other, where Bellafront sits asleep in a chair, under a taffata canopy." Here, unless we can take "passes" to mean "passes through," and understand accordingly that after Scudmore's exit by one of the regular doors, the rear-stage curtains draw, revealing Bellafront asleep, and that he reënters by the middle door, we are compelled to assume that action took place where action was impossible, namely, in the narrow passage leading to one of the two normal entering doors.[1]

Just one word more about this middle door. I am inclined to believe that Professor G. F. Reynolds has hit the nail on the head in arguing that, in all scenes where a door is indicated as leading from the lower stage to the balcony, particularly in scenes where it is locked or barred, the middle door is the one referred to. Professor Reynolds tells us that a conspicuous example is to be found in *The Maid's Tragedy*, I, 2.[2]

We come now to the nice question of the locking of the doors. Once upon a time I was of the opinion that no Elizabethan stage-door was ever really locked, that it was a matter of simple pretense; but maturer reflection, aided by greater knowledge, convinced me that this was wrong. In *Richard II*, act v, scene 3, we encounter a locked door with, first, the Duke of York, and then, his duchess pounding madly upon it; actions which (more especially if the door were of the valved order shown in the Swan drawing) could hardly have been performed unless the door were securely

---

[1] The situation is on a par with a similarly indicated change of locality in *Romeo and Juliet*, act 1, so ably elucidated by Mr. R. Crompton Rhodes in *Studies in the First Folio*, pp. 116, 117.

[2] *Modern Philology*, xii, no. 4, October 1914, p. 120; G. F. Reynolds on "William Percy and his Plays."

fastened. It must be admitted, however, that the evidence is somewhat contradictory; and it may be that in situations of a simpler order a mere pretense at locking sufficed. I remark that in Munday's *The Death of Robert, Earl of Huntington*, IV, I, a late sixteenth-century Rose play, Brand, as the direction has it, "seems to lock a door" proof that make-believe was occasionally employed. Many examples of scenes where the business of locking was performed, irrespective of the question whether locking really took place, could be cited; but it will suffice now to commend the student to *The Fatal Dowry*, II, I, and IV, I; *The Renegado*, IV, 2; *The Broken Heart*, IV, 4; *The Island Princess*, III, 3; *Lust's Dominion*, III, 2; *The Captain* IV, 4; and *The Spanish Gipsy*, I, 3. My own conclusions relative to the conventions of stage-door-locking, while in agreement with Reynolds's theory, extend a little beyond it. I am inclined to believe that, where only one door was locked, it was invariably the rear-stage door, and that, where the locking involved two doors, it was limited to the two normal doors of entrance. To have locked only a single front-stage door would have been foolishness. What we have to remember is that where the rear-stage door was locked, the outer doors were suppressed by convention. Here an apposite illustration is afforded by *The Captain*, IV, 5, the scene being in Lelia's House. My reading is that, at the opening of the scene, the disguised Father entered surreptitiously at the back, but after Lelia's appearance, the action must have been transferred to the front, so that Angelo, on the balcony, could witness what was taking place. Evidently the door subsequently locked by the Father (and unlocked by him later to allow Angelo to come on from above) was the rear-stage door. No outer door could have given the necessary illusion.

Unless the evidence of the Dutch sketch of the Swan is wholly misleading, it would appear that in the first two or three public theatres the two regulation entering doors faced the yard and stood flush in a perfectly straight wall. How long this system obtained, it would be difficult to say; but there are situations and stage directions in the early seventeenth-century drama which call for the use of oblique or opposite doors. Attention was first drawn to this point by the late William Archer in a newspaper article written in 1907,[1] much to the advance of our knowledge. Albright at once saw

[1] Illustrated article on "The Fortune Theatre, 1600," in *The Tribune* (London) for October 12, 1907, reproduced in the *Shakespeare Jahrbuch* for 1908, pp. 159 ff. The now familiar plans which inspired this article were drawn up by Mr. Walter H. Godfrey, F. S. A., at the instance and under the superintendence of William Archer, some months earlier, after a series of discussions in which I myself took part. A later article on the subject, written by Mr. Godfrey for *The Architectural Review*, was afterwards reprinted, with the designs, in Clapham and Godfrey's *Some Famous Buildings and Their Story* (1913).

WILLIAM ARCHER'S
CONJECTURAL ELIZABETHAN STAGE
WITH OBLIQUE DOORS

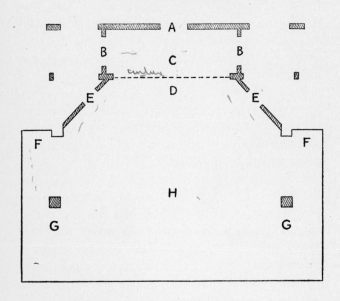

A = Middle, or third, entering door, leading from the tyring-house
to the inner stage.

B = Side entrances to inner stage.

C = Inner stage.

D = Curtains separating inner and outer stage.

E = Oblique side doors surmounted by boxes or balconies.

F = Outer-stage angles for people to stand in in the action unob-
served.

G = Pillars of the Heavens on public stages.

H = The outer stage.

the force of Archer's argument and bowed to it in depicting what he styled a typical Elizabethan stage, in the frontispiece to his book on *The Shakesperian Stage*.[1] Only one protest was made and that of no particular cogency. It was objected by Mr. Harold Child, who seems to have been laboring under the delusion that the curtains covered the doors as well as the rear stage, that oblique doors would have led to serious difficulties in the drawing of the curtains.[2] That this stricture had no validity can be readily seen by examining Archer's plan for an Elizabethan stage with oblique doors, drawn up by him some time subsequently but never published.[3]

It is only by a tortuous process of reasoning and by the collation of much minor detail that one can make approximation to the period when oblique doors were first introduced. For this purpose I have been to the pains to assemble a very considerable number of references to the use of opposite doors, both specific and implied, together with a number of stage directions dealing with a straight passage across the stage.

[1] Cf. Darrell Figgis, *Shakespeare*, pp. 91, 92, for some discussion of the subject.

[2] *Cambridge History of English Literature*, iv, 269 (chapter on "The Elizabethan Theatre").

[3] My acknowledgments are due to Lieutenant-Colonel Archer, William Archer's brother and executor, for his considerateness in supplying me with some copies of the plan for the purposes of this book.

Definite instructions for entrance by opposite doors are not to be found, I think, much before the close of the Jacobean period. In the 1622 quarto of *The Virgin Martyr*, a fairly recent Red Bull play, we have in act III, scene 3, "Enter Spungius and Hicius, ragged, at opposite doors." Here, as elsewhere, where the term "opposite" occurs, we are at a loss to determine whether the lower stage still had doors which were not opposite. Old stage directions are by no means remarkable for scientific precision: characters were sometimes said to "enter" when they were simply disclosed by the drawing of a curtain. It is not, however, until a somewhat later period that instructions for entry at opposite doors become fairly frequent. They are readily observable in Shirley's Cockpit plays: see *The Young Admiral*, III, 2; *The Humorous Courtier*, V, 2; and *Chabot, Admiral of France*, III, 2. In another Cockpit play, Ford's *The Lady's Trial*, we have at its opening, "Enter Piero and Futitle at opposite doors." Other evidence in Ford confirms the inference already deducible relative to the disposition of the doors at the old Drury Lane playhouse. It is reasonably assured that, no matter what the situation of the normal entering doors, and no matter which the theatre, they were always surmounted by balconies or windows. In Ford's *Love's Sacrifice*, another Caroline Cockpit play, there is a situation which calls for a balcony over an oblique door. In act v, we get the opening direction, "Enter above, Fiormonda, a Curtaine drawne, below is discovered Biancha in her night attire, leaning on a cushion at a table, holding Fernando by the hand." It is obvious that Fiormonda could not have witnessed the action taking place below had she been stationed at the extreme back of the stage.

Furthermore, we should take note that we get in Shirley, besides the references to opposite doors already spoken of, occasional directions for entry and exit at "opposite sides." Examples will be found in *The Gamester*, iii, 4, and iv, 1. This being likewise a Cockpit play, we cannot but assume that the implication is one simply of opposite doors.[1] That being so, we are at once afforded a clue to the provision of opposite doors much earlier in the century, seeing that we get directions in plays of its opening decade, not only for entry at opposite sides, but — what surely means the same thing — at opposite ends. Since the earliest of these occur in private-theatre plays, one becomes disposed to believe that the principle of opposite doors was of private-theatre origin and dated from the closing years of the sixteenth century. Ben Jonson makes

[1] For other entrances on "opposite sides," see *Nice Valour*, iii, 3; *A New Wonder, A Woman Never Vext*, act v; *The Guardian*, v, 3; *The Tale of a Tub*, iii, 1; Webster's *Appius and Virginia*, iii, 4, and v, 2; *The Duchess of Malfi*, ii, 1; Chapman's *Caesar and Pompey*, v, 2; and Rawlins's *The Rebellion*, iii, 2.

his characters come on from opposite sides at the opening of *Cynthia's Revels*, a Blackfriars play of 1600. Three years later, *The Malcontent* of Marston was produced at the same house,[1] and in act v, scene 2, a direction notifies us that Malevole and Maquerelle "enter from opposite sides . . . singing." That the Whitefriars, another private house, had opposite doors at a slightly later period, testimony of more than one kind establishes. To begin with, their presence is connoted by the action at the opening of Mason's *The Turk*, a piece brought out there in or about 1607. The direction runs, "Enter the Duke of Ferrara at one doore and the Duke of Venice at another doore, and mette at the midst of the stage." In a second Whitefriars play of the same period, *The Dumb Knight*, we get references in act i, scene 2, and act iv, scene 1, to entrances at "the one end . . . the other end."

But, if all this is to be taken as evidence of opposite doors, then at least one public theatre of the time had opposite doors, in view of the evidence advanced by the second part of Heywood's *If You Know not Me, You Know Nobody*, a play in all probability of Red Bull (certainly of public-theatre) origin. There is a certain juncture in this undivided piece where John and the Curtezan leave the stage for "another room," after which comes the direc-

---

[1] This play was shortly afterwards acted at the Globe by a different company, but the direction is evidence only for the original production.

tion, "Enter at the other end of the stage Hobs in his gown and slippers." Hobs crosses the stage and knocks at the door by which the two have just departed. But, if we are to assume on the strength of this evidence that the Red Bull in or about 1606 had opposite doors, then, by a parity of reasoning, we are forced to conclude that the Globe of a year or two earlier also had them, since in Jonson's *Sejanus*, v, 10, we get an entry on opposite sides. Two other items of evidence go to show that the Globe was equipped with opposite doors very early in the century; but their value is somewhat discounted by the fact that the texts which yield them are not in their original state. In *Troilus and Cressida*, v, 10, there is a stage direction running, "As Troilus is going out, enter from the other side, Pandarus." But *Troilus*, though written in 1601, remained unpublished until 1609, and meanwhile serious alteration of portions of the text had been made. The second item is afforded by *The Merry Devil of Edmonton*, a popular Globe play dating from the dawn of the century, but not published until 1608 and then from a corrupt copy. In act v, scene 2, the scene represents two neighboring inns whose signs have either been mischievously taken down or been transposed. We have to assume that the inns faced each other, instead of standing cheek by jowl, as the Host of the George refers to his trade rival as "mine overthwart neighbour." Hence, it is difficult to see how the position of the inns could have been fittingly conveyed save by signs placed above opposite doors.

Unfortunately, when we come to assemble the evidence for swift passages across the stage, it is not at all reassuring. Unless I very much mistake, it is all confined to the Caroline period, and, what is equally singular, to private-theatre plays. Typical examples occur in the opening scene of *The City Wit*, where a dinner is carried over the stage in covered dishes, and in the fourth act of *The Jovial Crew*, where "some beggars run over the stage." [1]

Assuredly this is not a subject on which to dogmatize, and now that I am compelled to sum up, I can give nothing better than my impressions. It would appear to me that opposite entering doors were first made use of when that most famous of all private theatres, the second Blackfriars, was opened, and that little by little the public theatres fell in line. Unfortunately, we do not know exactly when that event happened: it was certainly not later than the autumn of 1600, and it may have been as early as 1598. If the earlier date could be established, there would be good grounds for believing that the Globe was equipped with opposite doors from its inception.

Our attention is now free to concentrate on the

---

[1] See also Shirley's *Hyde Park*, III, 1; *A Cure for a Cuckold*, II, 2; *The Antipodes*, IV, 3 and 8; *The Loyal Subject*, IV, 2; *The Little French Lawyer*, III, 1; *The Chances*, V, 3; and *A Wife for a Month*, V, 1.

inner stage and its covering, a fruitful subject on which much that is new and true remains to be said. Profuse in its technicalities, the old theatrical world had more than one name for the one thing. What scholars require to grasp but never have been told is that the terms curtain, curtains, hangings, arras, traverse, and canopy all had precisely the same significance. Grave confusion has already arisen from lack of this knowledge. For example, Mr. R. Crompton Rhodes, in his thoughtful little book on *The Stagery of Shakespeare*,[1] attempts to draw a nice distinction between the Elizabethan import of "curtain" and "curtains," and would have us believe that, while the latter refers to the regulation covering of the inner stage, the former implies some temporary curtain specially rigged up for a particular purpose. There is not a tittle of evidence in support of this theory. It is obvious that a double curtain could be spoken of with equal fitness either in the singular or in the plural. I have compiled a representative list of examples where both terms are used, taking care not to confine my search to any particular period, and I defy any conscientious investigator to say, after he has examined the scenes in which they occur, that a single one of them has reference to anything save the covering of the rear stage.

For the term "curtain," see the prologue to *Cata-*

[1] Chap. 3, p. 32.

line; The Wisdom of Dr. Dodypoll, I, I; *Hoffman*, I, I, and IV, I; *The Fox*, I, I, and V, I; *The Faithful Shepherdess*, V, 2; *The Valiant Welshman*, V, 2; *News from Plymouth*, IV, study scene; *The Guardian*, III, 6; *Lust's Dominion*, I, I; *The Fatal Dowry*, II, 2; *The Mad Lover*, V, I; *The Seidge, or Love's Convert*, V, 8.

For "curtains," see the opening of *Friar Bacon and Friar Bungay*; also *A Warning for Fair Women*, II, I; the prologue to *The Merry Devil of Edmonton*; Marston's *The Wonder of Women, or Sophonisba*, V, I; *Grim the Collier of Croydon*, I, I; *2 Henry VI*, III, 2; *Lady Alimony*, I, I.

Before proceeding further, it is requisite to bear in mind that all Elizabethan stages, whether public or private, were equipped with two sets of curtains, the one immediately above the other. Surmounting the rear stage, on the first story of the tiring-house, was a moderate-sized room which was also covered with curtains. This I shall deal with later. What we now have to ask ourselves is, whether the stage was adorned with any other hangings besides these two sets of curtains. Hangings are frequently referred to in old plays, and a good deal of misconception is rife as to their nature. Because the stage was hung with black when a tragedy was performed, there is a prevailing idea that the whole of the tiring-house front was then covered with black hangings. The preposterousness of this concept becomes apparent once we come to give full consideration to the complex arrangement of the tiring-house front and to the necessity that all its varied parts should remain in sight. Look, for example, at Albright's frontispiece depicting his idea of a typical Elizabethan stage, or Mr. Noel Hills's map dealing with the same subject, and ask yourselves where, apart from the rear-stage and upper-stage openings, any such hangings could be placed. If we ponder the evidence demonstrating this draping of the stage with black when tragedies were to be performed, we cannot fail to see that all it really proves is that, when tragedy was to the fore, black silk or cloth was substituted for the tapestry curtains which normally shrouded both the rear stage and the upper room. No exercise of ingenuity can twist it to convey anything more. In *A Warning for Fair Women*, Tragedy, after triumphing over her rivals in the induction, appears throughout the play as Chorus. At the opening of the second act we find her saying:

> Till now you have but sitten to behold
> The fatal entrance to our bloody scene;
> And by gradation seen how we have grown
> Into the main stream of our tragedy.
> All wee have done hath only been in words:
> But now we come unto the dismal act,
> *And in these sable curtains shut we up*
> The comic entrance to our direful play.

This shows at least that the lower-stage curtains were black when the speech was delivered. What

investigators have failed to see, however, is that
there is nothing in any of the divers other references,
direct and metaphorical, to what Marston styles
the "Black-visaged shows" of tragedy,[1] warranting a more general draping with black. A double
set of sable curtains would quite well have answered
when Truth said, in the induction to Yarrington's
Two Lamentable Tragedies in One,

> Our stage doth weare habilliments of woe.

One much-used old metaphor, based on Tragedy's
black garb, has proved a frequent stumbling-block
to the Shakespearean commentator. My earliest
trace of it is in Sidney's *Arcadia*:

> There arose even with the sun a veil of dark clouds, before
> his face, had blacked all over the face of heaven, preparing
> as it were a mournful stage for a tragedy to be played on.

This, I think, proved a general source of inspira-
tion. One traces the idea in the opening speech of
1 King Henry VI, beginning with "Hung be the
Heavens with black," etc. The allusion here is
best elucidated by a later variant in *The Insatiate
Countess*, IV, 5:

> The stage of heaven is hung with solemn black,
> A time best fitting to act tragedies.

But Shakespearean commentators have per-
versely elected to ignore the obvious meaning, and
with misguided ingenuity have chosen to believe

---

[1] Prologue to *Antonio's Revenge*.

that the heavens Shakespeare was thinking of was "the heavens" of the playhouse. Hence they deduce for us quite an astonishing theatrical arrangement. I need quote only from Sir Sidney Lee,[1] who, in writing of "the slanting canopy of thatch" called the heavens, tells us that "the tapestry hangings were suspended from the covering, at some height from the stage, but well within view of the audience."[2] This is mere guesswork, and unworthy of any credence. It will suffice, I think, to say that in the entire corpus of the Elizabethan drama, using the term in its broadest sense, there is only a single reference to hangings which admits of an interpretation otherwise than to stage curtains, and it occurs in a late Caroline play. In Davenant's Blackfriars tragedy, *The Unfortunate Lovers*, act v, hangings are drawn twice in succession to show severally the bodies of Calrotto and Amaranta. Seeing that no instance can be found elsewhere of hangings being drawn, it would seem that the term was rather clumsily applied to the lower-stage curtains. There is only one difficulty: unless but one half of the curtains was opened at a time, it is impossible to see how the effect could have been procured by rear-stage means.

[1] *Life of William Shakespeare* (American edit., 1916), p. 76.

[2] See also J. Churton Collins, *Posthumous Essays*, 11; T. S. Graves on "Night Scenes in the Elizabethan Theatres," *Englische Studien*, xlvii (1913), 64, 65, and my reply, *ibid.*, xlviii, 214–216.

No other reference to the hangings affords any puzzlement. They all apply, or, to speak by the card, can be readily shown to apply, to the stage curtains. I can do no more than examine a few examples. In *The Staple of News*, v, 1, we have the direction, "P. jun. makes a sign to Tho., who retires behind the hangings." He retires to listen.[1] Here the rear-stage curtains are indicated, since the conventional hiding-place was behind them. "Behind the arras" meant practically the same thing. This clue to the sense in which Jonson uses the term "hangings" helps to an understanding of the passage in his address "to the Reader," prefixed to *The New Inn*, in which he showers down contempt on those who came

to possess the stage against the play . . . and by their confidence of rising between the acts in oblique lines, make affidavitt to the whole house of their not understanding one scene. Armed with this prejudice, as the stage furniture, or arras clothes, they were there: for the faces in the hangings, and they, beheld alike.

Other references to the faces in the hangings show that normally the hangings were tapestries or

[1] Cf. *The Noble Gentleman*, iv, 5, where, on Longueville speaking without, Beaufort gestures to Maria and says, "the hangings," meaning that she is to hide herself behind them. In *The Northern Lass*, iv, 3, Holdup similarly "withdraws behind the hangings." In Davenant's *News from Plymouth*, iv, Wormell refers to the hangings as the haunt of eavesdroppers. In *The Wits* of the same author, references *passim* to "the hangings" can safely be taken to refer to the rear-stage curtains.

painted cloths.[1] Take the curious scene in Day's
Law Tricks, or Who would have thought it, III, I,
where, on the approach of Polymetes and Julio,
Count Lurdo acts on the advice of Emilia and hides
behind the hangings. These are subsequently de-
scribed by Emilia as representing "Venus kissing
Adonis in the violet bed." Polymetes lays a wager
with Julio that he will hit Venus's pap at three
passes, and this so frightens the Count that the
arras begins to tremble. The "business" of the
scene is lost, but it would appear that Lurdo evidently figures somehow as Vulcan in the scene.

Then again, in a much later play, Mayne's *The
City Match*, II, 3, we get the following revealing
colloquy: —

Aurelia.   O prodigy, to hear an image speak!
　　　　　Why sir, I took you for a mute i' th' hangings.
　　　　　I'll tell the faces.
　　Tim.   Gentlemen, do I
　　　　　Look like one of them Trojans?[2]
　　Aur.   'T is so; your face
　　　　　Is missing here, sir; pray, step back again,
　　　　　And fill the number. You, I hope, have more
　　　　　Truth in you than to fetch yourself away,
　　　　　And leave my room unfurnish'd.

In Shirley's *The Bird in a Cage*, IV, 2, much capi-
tal is likewise made out of the stage hangings. The

---

[1] For painted cloths, see *Shakespeare's England*, ii, 129, 130.

[2] The Trojan War was a favorite subject for old tapestries. See
Shakespeare's England, II, 9, 10; also the illustrations to Sir Sidney
Colvin's article in *A Book of Homage to Shakespeare*.

byplay is played to the faces in the arras, referred to punningly as "our mixed audience of silk and crewel gentlemen in the hangings." [1]   Note that this was the second time that Shirley had pressed the stage fittings into dramatic service. In *The Traitor*, act III, Depazzi, fearing eavesdroppers, "takes up the hangings"; and later on he says, "I do not like that face in the arras; on my conscience he points at me." It is evident from this, *The Traitor* being a tragedy, that in later Caroline times the stage was no longer draped with black when the sterner muse held the boards.

The custom of calling for the author on the *première* of a new play had its inception in Paris in the mid-eighteenth century, and was not followed in England until about the third decade of the century following. But in Pre-Restoration times, the fortunes of a new piece could be estimated by the heartiness or the tepidity of the applause which followed upon the epilogue-speaker's indirect appeal for the opinion of the house. Hence, it became the custom, on first days, for the author to stand hidden within the tiring-house, that he might at once learn his fate. A number of allusions in old plays to this practice goes to show that the arras and the hangings and the curtains were merely so

[1] Cf. Cartwright, *The Ordinary*, III, 3, where Priscilla the maid asks Meanwell to amuse himself with the "pretty stories in the hangings" until she acquaints her mistress of his presence.

many names for the one thing. To begin with, we have the similitude in Fletcher's *The Woman Hater*, ii, 1:

> There is no poet acquainted with more shakings and quakings towards the latter end of his new play, when he's in that case that he stands peeping between the curtains, so fearfully, that a bottle of ale cannot be opened, but he thinks somebody hisses.

Later references testify to the same practice in slightly different terms. In the induction to Jonson's *Bartholomew Fair*, we find the Stage Keeper saying:

> But for the whole play, will you have the truth on 't? I am looking, lest the poet hear me, or his man, Master Brome, behind the arras — it is like to be a very conceited scurvy one, in plain English.

The Master Brome here referred to afterwards himself turned playwright, and in the epilogue to his comedy, *The English Moor*, says of himself:

> Nor studies he the art to have it said,
> He skulks behind the hangings as afraid
> Of a hard censure, or pretend to brag
> Here's all your money again brought in i' th' bag.

Assuredly, the dramatist who, in his epilogue, offered the audience their money back if they disliked his play, was asking for trouble. But it would appear from Brome's gird that one of the aristocratic dilettanti of his time had assured the public that money was his last consideration when he took his pen in hand. If, however, Brome disdained to await the verdict on his play unseen, he was probably the exception among professional Caroline dramatists. When Shirley's *The Duke's Mistress* was brought out in 1636, the epilogue told the house that "the poet stands listening behind the arras, to hear what will become of his new play."

I see now that I was over-cautious when at an earlier juncture I expressed some doubts as to whether the hangings drawn at the Blackfriars in 1638 in the fifth act of Davenant's *The Unfortunate Lovers* could have been in reality the rear-stage curtains. A reference to the hangings in the prologue to the play clearly shows that Davenant used the term to imply stage curtains. The author was represented as saying that the Caroline audience had grown more fastidious than the audience of a score of years previously:

> For they, he swears, to th' theatre would come,
> Ere they had din'd, to take up the best room;
> There sit on benches, not adorn'd with mats,
> And graciously did vail their high-crown'd hats
> To every half-dress'd player, as he still
> Through the hangings peep'd to see how the house did fill.[1]

The reference, obviously, is to central hangings, and the only hangings that could have been at once central and divided were the stage curtains.

[1] Cited from the quarto of 1643. A slightly different version of the prologue is given in the Davenant Folio of 1673, p. 299; *e.g.*, the last quoted line there reads, "Through Hangings peep'd to see the Gall'ries fill."

And just here, let me say, I find in Ben Jonson's translation of Horace's *De Arte Poetica* a passage which throws curious light on old-time play-house procedure. It is as follows:

> Here what it is the people and I desire:
> If such a one's applause thou dost require,
> That tarries till the hangings be ta'en down,
> And sits till th' epilogue says 'clap or crown:'
> The customs of each age thou must observe,
> And give their years and natures, as they swerve
> Fit rights.

I have a note of having read somewhere that Jonson's version of the *De Arte Poetica* is very close —what Dryden called a metaphrase in contradistinction to a paraphrase. With that opinion few scholars will agree: it is certainly not borne out by the lines just cited.[1] Jonson was here struggling to translate

> Si plausoris eges aulaea manentis, et usque
> Sessuri, donec cantor, vos plaudite, dicat;
> Aetatis cuiusque notandi sunt tibi mores,
> Mobilibusque decor naturis dandus, et annis.

---

[1] Jonson's translation was published in 1640, in 12mo. Variant MSS exist. Jonson also gives

> "Nor must the foole, that would hope the fate
> Once seen, to be again call'd for, and play'd,
> Have more or less than just five acts,"

for

> "Neve minor quinto, neu sit productior actu
> Fabula, quae posci vult, et spectata reponi.

This modernization does not give much support to the now fashionable theory that Shakespeare did not write his plays in acts.

But, in the absence of any analogue to the Roman *aulaeum* — that curious curtain which descended at the beginning of the play and rose at its close [1] — in the Elizabethan theatre, he could render the first line only by a far-fetched reference to the hangings. The historical investigator, however, has reason to rejoice over his difficulty. If the hangings had not operated as curtains, there would have been little sense in lugging them in. It is noteworthy, moreover, that this is the only reference we have in all Elizabethan literature to the daily removal of the hangings after the play. Possibly that practice was confined to the public stages, where it would have been impolitic to let more or less costly tapestries and painted cloths remain permanently *in situ*, a prey to the damp.

After what has been already said, it may seem a work of supererogation for me to proceed to demonstrate that the arras and the hangings were the same thing, but we are breaking new ground, digging up new facts, and while in pursuit of such a task no evidence can be deemed negligible. It will be recalled that in the induction to *Cynthia's Revels*, a private-theatre play of 1600, one of the three children proceeds to imitate a sober-minded gallant coming to the play, and, on being begged to take a seat on the stage, says:

[1] For which, see Lawrence, *The Elizabethan Playhouse*, 1st Ser., p. 112.

Away, wag; what, wouldst thou make an implement of me? 'Slid, the boy takes me for a piece of perspective,[1] I hold my life, or some silk curtain, come to hang the stage here. Sir crack, I am none of your fresh pictures, that use to beautify the decayed arras in a public theatre.

This is a puzzling speech over which many have stumbled; but, although it would appear that the private-theatre stage at this period had a monopoly of silk curtains, it were idle to infer from that monopoly that neither arras nor painted cloths were in use then on the private-theatre stage. Within a decade we get evidence to the contrary. Produced, as I take it, about 1609, *The Knight of the Burning Pestle* was undoubtedly a private-theatre play. In one of the intervals between the acts, we find the Citizen's Wife asking, "Now, sweet lamb, what story is that painted upon the cloth? The confutation of St. Paul?" And her husband replies: "No, lamb, that's Ralph and Lucrece." But, of course, a good many changes may have taken place in the course of nine years. Apparently, however, it took more than twice nine before the public theatre began to indulge in the luxury of silk curtains. In John Tatham's little book of verse, *Fancies Theatre*, published in 1640, is a prologue written for the

---

[1] Absurdly taken by some commentators to refer to, and prove the contemporary use of, stage scenery. Here Jonson can best be elucidated by himself. Carlo Buffone, in *Every Man Out*, IV, 3, l. 2850, says, "I brought some dozen or twentie gallants this morning to view him (as you'ld doe a piece of perspective) in at a key-hole." Accordingly, a piece of perspective was a peep-show.

Fortune Players on their recent removal to the Red Bull, which begins:

> Here, gentlemen, our anchor's fixt; and we
> Disdaining *Fortune's* mutability,
> Expect your kind acceptance; then we'll sing
> (Protected by your smiles, our ever-spring)
> As pleasant as if we had still possest
> Our lawfull portion out of Fortune's breast.
> Only we would require you to forbear
> Your wonted custom, band(y)ing tile and pear
> Against our *curtains*, to allure us forth;
> I pray, take notice, these are of more worth;
> Pure Naples silk, not worsted.

This appeal — half a boast — would not have been very apposite had the use of silk curtains on the public-theatre stage then been usual.

If, for a moment, we assume that the hangings or arras were separate from the stage curtains, an extra feature, it is reasonably assured that, beyond the spaces covered by the two sets of curtains, there was no part of the tiring-house front where they could be so hung that sufficient room would be left for characters to hide, or good-sized properties to be placed, behind them. Yet of such hiding and such placing we have an abundance of evidence. Falstaff's bulk here serves us in good stead. In *2 Henry IV*, ii, 4, the Prince finds the fat knight snoring behind the arras, which, in this case, must surely be equated with the rear-stage curtains, since the searching of the obese one's pockets would have demanded some elbow-room. Moreover, in *The*

Merry Wives of Windsor, Falstaff more than once ensconces himself behind the arras: a lucky circumstance, seeing that the happy variability of the quarto and the folio texts reveals to us exactly where the arras was situated. In the quarto version of act IV, scene 2, Mrs. Ford, on Mrs. Page's approach, says, "Step behind the arras, good Sir John"; but in the folio version of the scene she asks him to "step into th' chamber," which practically means to hide himself behind the rear-stage curtains.[1]

A similar proof of position is to be found in the fifth act of Chapman's *Revenge of Bussy D'Ambois,* where the Guise "takes up the arras," as about to depart to the Council, "and the Guard enters upon him" to do the bloody deed. They could not have confronted him unless the arras had covered the rear-stage. So, too, in *Bussy D'Ambois,* the play to which the *Revenge* was a sequel, we have evidence of the custom of placing properties immediately behind the arras, so that they might be ready to hand for use in a coming scene. In act I, scene I, occurs the prompter's warning, "Table, Chessboard and Tapers behind the arras."

[1] Note the theatrical metaphor in the fourth act of *Epicoene:* "You two shall be the chorus behind the arras, and whip out between the acts and speak." In *If You Know not Me, You Know Nobody,* II, Phillip hides behind the arras, whence he speaks aside. In Thomas Jordan's *The Walks of Islington and Hodgson,* I, 2, is some curious stage business in which, incidentally "Splend. stands within the arras."

But the clearest proof that the arras and the rear-stage curtains were identical lies in directions for the drawing of the arras to make discoveries. In *Tamburlaine the Great, Part II*, act II, scene 4, we read that "The Arras is drawen, and Zenocrate lies in her bed of state Tamburlaine sitting by her: three Phisitians about her bed, tempering potions." Similarly, in that highly mysterious play, *Sir Thomas More*, we have in act I, scene 2, according to the latter-day divisions, "An arras is drawne, and behinde it (as in sessions) sit the L. Maior, Iustice Suresbie and other Justices; Sheriffe Moore and the other Sherife sitting by." A much later example is to be found in Ford's *The Lover's Melancholy*, II, 2, where Cleophila "draws the arras" and reveals the slumbering Meleander.

It is remarkable that the term "Traverse," notwithstanding its neat applicability to the rear-stage curtains, is only so applied four times in the whole corpus of the Elizabethan drama. Yet, methinks, it was in commoner use than this implies. Early in the sixteenth century, the term was mostly associated with the screens formed of curtains put up in chapels, halls, and large rooms. The traverse was a common adjunct of court ceremonial, and was always utilized at the formal reception of ambassadors. The term implied something that drew across, and the curtain or curtains to which it applied were invariably attached to metal rings running on an iron rod. In this we have a description, in brief, of the traverses of the Elizabethan stage; no other kind of curtain was known in the Pre-Restoration playhouse. Of the early sense in which the term was used, we have an instance in Skelton's *The Bowge of Courte*:

> Of one and other that wolde this lady see;
> Which sat behynde a traves of sylke fyne. [1]

Close on a century later, we find Daniel writing in his *Civil Wars:*

> He drawes a Trauerse 'twixt his greeuances:
> Lookes like the time: his eye made no report
> Of what he felt within.[2]

Rare as is our trace of the vocable in early stage parlance, its intermittent application to the rear-stage curtains serves to show that the rear stage was a heritage from the private indoor entertainment of the pre-theatrical period. This fact becomes apparent once we examine the interlude of *Godly Queene Hester*, which dates from before 1561, the year in which it was printed. Here, one notes that, immediately after the delivery of the prologue, King Ahasuerus is discovered "sitting in a chaire, speaking to his counsell." But more positive indications of the use of a curtain are given later, especially in the two stage directions, "Here the Kynge entreth the traverse and Hardy-dardy entreth the place,"

---

[1] Prol., 57, 58.   [2] Book VIII.

and "Here the kynge entryth the travers and Aman goeth out." [1]

There is hardly any early stage technicality about which there has been so much fruitless controversy as the term "canopy." [2] I do not know whether the arrangement of the rear-stage front in the private theatres differed in anywise from its arrangement in the public theatres — it might be that in the private houses it projected somewhat; but the fact remains, whatever be its significance, that the use of the term canopy in early stage directions is strictly confined to private-theatre plays. Notwithstanding the prevalent doubt as to its meaning, I think it is possible to demonstrate that the term was one of the many names bestowed upon the rear-stage curtains. In the Third Quarto of *Bussy D'Ambois*, published in 1641, we have at the close of act v, scene 2, the stage direction: "He [Montsurry] puts the [dead body of the] Frier in the vault [down a trap] and follows. She [the wounded Tamyra] raps her self in the arras."

Two scenes later, in the same quarto, comes a connective direction: "Thunder. Intrat Umbra

[1] For later uses of the term "traverse," see Chambers, *The Eliz. Stage*, iii, 25, 26.

[2] See C. W. Wallace, *The Children of the Chapel at Blackfriars*, p. 48 (where the term is explained as meaning a sort of movable three- or four-sided tent); T. S. Graves, *The Court and the London Theatres during the reign of Elizabeth*, pp. 5, 12, 14, 16, 17, 88, 89; Chambers, *The Eliz. Stage*, ii, 557.

Frier and discovers Tamyra"; but it is noteworthy that in the two earlier quartos, both published over thirty years previously, the equivalent
direction tells us that the Friar's ghost "discovers
Tamyra wrapt in a canapie." From all of which
the inference would be that "canopy" = arras.

In Marston's *The Wonder of Women, or Sophonisba*, IV, I, representing the exterior of a cave, we
read that "a treble Viall and a base lute play softly
within the canopy"; and at the end of the act we
are told that "Syphax hastneth within the canopy
as to Sophonisba's bed." In the scene which follows (V, I) evidently it is the bed-curtains, and not
the curtains of the rear-stage, which Syphax opens
in order to view his bedfellow. More important
still is the evidence in Heminges' Caroline Cockpit
play, *The Fatal Contract*. In act V, scene 2, we read,
"Enter the Eunuch . . . solemnly drawes the
Canopie, where the Queen sits at one end bound
with Landrey at the other, both as asleep"; and,
a little later in the scene, we are told that the
Eunuch "draws the curtain again." In other words,
he first opened the stage curtains and then closed
them again. Here "canopie" = curtain, so that
already we have proof that canopy, arras, and curtain all meant the same thing.

There was another sense in which canopy was
then used — in its plainer and commoner significa-
tion of an awning or overhead covering; and it

is unfortunate that Davenant uses the word in both senses, since investigators have thereby been much confused. In act III, scene 2, of his *The Just Italian*, Scoperta is revealed sitting under a canopy. This canopy was evidently part of a chair of state, as she speaks of it as "this chair." The meaning here is, I think, made apparent by the action in act I, scene 2, of Massinger's *The Picture*, where a procession comes on with Honoria in the midst under a canopy of state. Elsewhere, however, Davenant employs both "canopy" and "arras" when he wants to indicate the rear-stage curtains. In the folio version of *The Platonick Lovers*, a canopy is drawn in the second act, revealing Eurithea lying on a couch. So, too, in *Albovine*, v, 3, we have, at the opening, a direction running: "A Canopy is drawn, the King is discover'd sleeping over Papers: enter Paradine with his sword drawn." Paradine evidently enters in front by one of the two normal entering doors. In reference to him, a subsequent direction reads: "He puts him [that is, the King] behind the arras, opens the door. Enter Rhodolinda." The door he opened was evidently at the back of the rear stage, what was known as "the middle door." Later, when the King is awakened, he seems to have come forward: the text shows that he goes mad and dies. Then knocking is heard, and Paradine hides the body on the rear stage and closes the curtains. Subsequently he tells

Rhodolinda of the King's death, and "opes the arras" in confirmation. He then stabs her to death, and "carries her in," with the reflection, "what a full Sepulcher is this." Throughout all this action he never disappears from sight. Later on, "he draws the Arras and discovers Albovine, Rhodolinda, Valdaura, dead in chairs." I submit that it is impossible to visualize the action in this stirring act unless one assumes that the canopy and the arras are convertible terms and both signify the rear-stage curtains.

Apparently, it was not the office of any stage official such as the bookholder or tireman, and of him alone, to attend regularly to the opening and closing of the curtains. There were undoubtedly occasions when the duty was performed by some stage hand, but in the generality of cases, it fell to the lot of the players themselves. Beginning with *Doctor Faustus*, one readily recalls several old plays in which the Prologue opened the action by drawing the curtains. Malone points out that "when King Henry VIII is to be discovered by the Dukes of Suffolk and Norfolk, reading in his study, the scenical direction in the First Folio, 1623 (which was printed apparently from playhouse copies), is 'The King draws the curtain and sits reading pensively.'"[1]

I was once told by an eminent Shakespearean

[1] Malone's *Shakespeare*, (Dublin, 1794), ii, 62, 63, note 9, where other examples are also cited.

scholar, now dead, that he was convinced there was some blunder in this direction, since it was not in keeping for a king to perform such an office; but he forgot that it was the player, and not the king, who performed it, and that it was performed unseen of the audience. Had it not been that, like some other Shakespearean scholars, he had no great acquaintance with the minor Elizabethan drama, he would have known that it was quite a common thing for players in full sight of the audience to open and close the curtains. No stage king possibly ever demeaned himself thus, but at least one earl forgot his coronet. In *Westward Hoe*, we get a direction, "While the song is heard, the Earle drawes a Curten, and sets forth a Banquet." Occasional parallels of the king's action in *Henry VIII* are to be found. In *Lust's Dominion*, with the opening of the play, four characters enter smoking, followed by the Queen of Spain and two pages. Then we are told that "Eleazer sitting on a chair, suddenly draws the curtain." This sounds to me an extraordinary acrobatic feat: I cannot guess how it was accomplished.[1] What it reveals to us is that, notwithstanding the apparently rudimentary method of manipulation, the double curtain could be neatly and quickly removed. A few other direc-

[1] For other examples of players' drawing the curtains either from the back or the front, see *The Woman Hater*, v, 1, *What You Will*, acts II (twice) and v, *The Lover's Progress*, III, 1, *The Guardian*, III, 6, *The Mad Lover*, v, 1, *News from Plymouth*, IV, 2.

tions testify to the same effect. In the opening scene of *Grim the Collier of Croydon*, after St. Dunstan has lain down to sleep, comes the direction, "Lightning and thunder; the curtains drawn on a sudden; Pluto, Minos, Aecus, Rhadamanthus, set in counsel; before them Malbecco's ghost guarded with furies." Again, in the course of the Masque of Statues, in the fifth act of Cartwright's, *The Siedge, or Love's Convert* (a play first printed in 1651, eight years after the author's death), "the Curtain flies aside," to disclose five ladies on pedestals.

There is some slight reason for believing that the curtains were always opened at the beginning of a play, whether or no the opening action was on the rear stage; and there is, on the whole, somewhat better reason for believing that the curtains were always closed at the end of the performance. To prove either custom would be to prove both, since the existence of the one would connote the other. The point is not as trivial as it looks, because, assuming the dual practice, it would undoubtedly have had some influence upon dramatic construction. There would have been a tendency to open and close the play with rear-stage action. But at no period can I find evidence of the sway of any strict principle bearing on the subject. There were occasional early plays, like *Doctor Faustus*, as I have already pointed out, in which the prologue drew the curtains at the close of his speech; and there were other early plays, like *The Case is Altered* and *Lust's Dominion*, in which, although we have no trace of the Prologue so doing, the action opened on the rear stage. A theatrical metaphor employed by Massinger in *The Guardian* seems to indicate the initial withdrawal of the curtains in Caroline times. In act III, scene 6, Severino, after giving Calipso a few preliminary slashes with a knife, says ominously:

> This is but an induction; I will draw
> The curtains of the tragedy hereafter.

Possibly we should not greatly err in drawing a conclusion applicable at least to the period, from this phrasing: theatrical metaphors had of necessity to be based upon matters of common knowledge.

The evidence for the closing of the curtains at the end is somewhat fuller and perhaps more convincing. To begin with, we have the reference in the lines, printed without attribution in 1612 and since ascribed to Sir Walter Raleigh, which ring the changes on the eternal "all the world's a stage" theme:

> What is our life? The play of passion.
> Our mirth? The music of division:
> Our mothers' wombs the tiring houses be,
> Where we are dressed for Life's short comedy.
> The earth the stage; Heaven the spectator is,
> Who sits and views whoso'er doth act amiss.
> The graves which hide us from the searching sun
> Are like drawn curtains when the play is done.
> Thus playing post we to our latest rest,
> And then we die in earnest, not in jest.

At a later period, Henry King, Bishop of Chichester, wrote "A Dirge," which was published with his *Poems* in 1657, consisting of six stanzas in which the life of man is compared to a storm, a flower, a dream, a dial, and a play. It ends with:

> It is a weary interlude,
> Which doth short joys, long woes include;
> The world the stage, the prologue tears:
> The acts vain hope and varied fears;
> The scene [1] shuts up with loss of breath,
> And leaves no epilogue but death.

Finally, we find Drummond of Hawthornden writing in his *Cypress Grove* in 1649: "Every one cometh there to act his part of the tragi-comedy, called life, which done, the courtain is drawn and he removing is said to die." [2]

To-day, lucidity must be gained at all hazards, and scholars speak glibly of the rear stage or inner stage, ignoring the fact that such terms were never employed during the platform-stage era. It is important for us to note that, apart from reference by implication, the only term applied throughout its existence to this portion of the tiring-house was "the study," since the term itself suggests that the

---

[1] Cf. *Volpone or the Fox*, v, 6, which opens with a discovery, and ends with "The Scene closes"; *The Jovial Crew*, I, 1, "He opens the scene; the beggars are discover'd in their postures, etc," and again in II, 1, "Randal opens the scene. The Beggars discovered at their feast."

[2] Cf. T. S. Graves in "Notes in Elizabethan Theatres," in *Studies in Philology*, xiii (1916), 120, 121.

place was almost wholly reserved for the staging of interiors. Be that as it may, one thing is certain: wherever we get mention of the study in stage directions, it connotes rear-stage action. Dyce failed to grasp this when striving to elucidate the sequence of directions in Greene's *Honourable History of Friar Bacon and Friar Bungay:* "Bacon and Edward go into the study. . . . Enter Margaret and Friar Bongay." All he could do was to proffer the suggestion that "perhaps a curtain or traverse, put up for the occasion at the back of the stage, was withdrawn, and discovered Margaret and Bungay (who are afterwards joined by Lucy and the Devil), and when the representation in the glass was supposed to be over, the curtain was drawn back again." Unfortunately, Elizabethan investigators have not yet got out of this old facile habit of solving intricate problems of staging by rigging up temporary curtains in all sorts of possible and impossible places. But, in Greene's play, as elsewhere where the term is used, the word "study" clearly localizes the action. It is almost invariably to be taken in its technical, not its literal sense. Sometimes the place to which it is applied is merely a store room,[1] and sometimes a room in a hotel.[2] The instances where

[1] *The Devil's Law Case,* IV, 2.

[2] *The Life and Death of Lord Cromwell,* III, 2 (Tucker Brooke's division in *The Shakespeare Apocrypha*). For other uses of the term, see *ibid.,* II, 1, and IV, 5; *Hamlet,* First Quarto, scene vi: "Yourself and I will stand close in the study" (rendered in Second Quarto and

it indicates something otherwise than the rear stage are so few as to be negligible. Personally, I know of only two. In *Titus Andronicus*, v, 2, in both Quarto and Folio, the scene evidently opens below. "Enter Tamora and her two sons disguised. . . . They knocke and Titus opens his studie door." Brodmeier thinks that Titus appeared above at a window, but whether that was so or not, he certainly appeared above, for Tamora asks him to "come down and welcome me." It is noteworthy that in the analogous scene in the German version of the play,[1] Titus first looks down, then speaks, and finally descends.

But mention of a study door does not necessarily localize the study. The only real exception to the rule occurs in *Epicoene, or The Silent Woman*, iv, 2, where two small studies (or closets), with doors, were required at either end of the stage. This is a Jacobean private-theatre play, and the staging of the scene remains to me a mystery. I do not think that action ever took place in the passages leading to the two regular entrances; yet, unless we assume

Folio as "behind the arras"); *Satiromastix*, i, 2; *Poetaster*, i, 1; *Cataline*, i, 1; *The Woman Hater*, v, 1 (where the opening of the curtains locates the study); *The Divil's Charter*, i, 4, and iv, 1 and 5; *Ram Alley*, i, 2; *The Virgin Martir*, ii, 1; *'Tis Pity She's a Whore*, ii, 1, and iii, 6; *The Fair Maid of the Inn*, iv, 2; *The Fair Maid of the Exchange*, v, 5; *The Novella*, i, 2; *The Maid's Revenge*, iii, 2; *The Staple of News*, ii, 5 (a puzzling scene, unless the significance of "the study" is fully grasped).

[1] For which see Albert Cohn, *Shakespeare in Germany*, p. 225.

that the two entering doors answered for the studies, it is impossible to visualize the action. The only way out of the difficulty would be to postulate that by 1609 the private theatre had opposite doors of entrance, and that the old doors in the tiring-house front still remained and were put to other purposes. The fact that later directions so often specify entrances by opposite doors would imply that the stage had doors which were not opposite.

In the public theatre, where performances were given in the afternoon and by natural light, time for many months in the year had to be rigidly economized. The study was essentially a time-saving device. It enabled an elaborately staged scene, a scene demanding a litter of properties, to be got ready for use while action in front was proceeding. Properties were frequently placed in position on the front stage, in full sight of the audience, but only such as could be easily handled and quickly removed. In nearly all cases where cumbrous properties were required by the action their place was on the rear stage. Because of the time available for the setting of the study and the number of things that could be placed in position, the study admitted of superior pictorial illusiveness, inasmuch as by its means the players could procure the atmosphere of a richly furnished interior. Note, for example, the description of Sharkino's sanctum in *The Maid's Revenge*, III, 2, which, according to a

direction, was "furnished with glasses, phials, pictures of wax character, wands, conjuring habit,
powders and painting." Being Shirley's, this, of
course, was a Caroline play, but the gratefulness of
the study as a means of elaborate mounting had been
discovered at a much earlier period. In the fourth
act of Sharpham's *The Fleire*, an early Jacobean
play, we have the direction: "Enter Signior Alunio
the Apothecarie in his shop with his wares about
him" — one of the many curious instances where
a disclosure is stated in terms of entrance.

It is noteworthy that, among early investigators
of the Elizabethan stage, Ludwig Tieck was the
first to postulate the existence of the rear stage.[1]
According to his view, it was placed at an elevation
and approached by steps. Since his day, belief in
an elevated rear stage has occasionally been reite-
rated, though no supporter of the hypothesis has
been able to advance any material evidence in
justification of that belief. Personally, I know of
only one solitary theatrical situation that would
seem to demand an elevated rear stage; but as it
happens, it occurs in a play which, although certainly acted, was never acted in a theatre. This was
Quarles's *The Virgin Widow*, a comedy printed in
1649, some years after the author's death, with the
intimation that it had been privately acted at
Chelsea by a number of young gentlemen. In act

---

[1] In his novel, *Der Junge Tischlermeister*.

iv, scene 2, Quibble the mountebank, while standing on a scaffold, delivers an harangue in the midst of which he "drawes a Curtaine, and discovers his shop furnisht." The position certainly seems to require an elevated rear stage, but we have no means of knowing whether it was devised in accord with the arrangement of any late Caroline playhouse. But I may say, after having long cogitated over the matter, that there are sundry fatal objections to Tieck's theory. Heavy properties, such as beds and scaffolds, were often thrust out from the rear stage, and it is impossible to see how this could have been done if the rear stage were connected with the front stage by steps. That necessity seems to have overridden all other demands, else an elevated rear stage would not have been without its particular gratefulness. In throne scenes, it would have provided a ready-made dais, and it would also have had some convenience in senate scenes.

Knowledge of Elizabethan stage matters is acquired only by inches. Almost a score of years ago, Professor A. C. Bradley, in his memorable Oxford lectures on poetry, gave it as his opinion that the sides of the rear stage were open to the view.[1] That hypothesis proved highly acceptable to so cautious and sane-minded an investigator as the late William Archer, who wrote, in an unpublished note now in my possession:

[1] *Oxford Lectures on Poetry* (1909), p. 379 n.

A little reflection will show us that in all probability (since
bulky "properties" had often to be placed upon and removed
from it) access to the rear stage would be as little obstructed
as possible. Thus there is every reason to suppose that it
was not in any true sense of the word a "niche" or "alcove,"
but rather a corridor, some six or seven feet deep and open
at each end. Nor can we see any reason to doubt that there
would be a large door in the middle of its back wall. Why
should the Elizabethan playwright have denied himself such
an obvious convenience? And, apart from stage directions
naming, or clearly pointing to, a "Middle" door, we conceive
that this door was habitually used to figure the gate of a town
or castle, of which the Upper Stage had served as the battle-
ments. For example, it was probably by the Middle Door
that Henry V entered Harfleur. The two other doors had
been used for other entrances; it would have been absurd
for the Rear Stage curtains to figure the gates of a town; and
for Henry and his army to go off by one of the side-entrances
to the Rear Stage, would have been, in the circumstances,
wholly ineffective.

I have quoted this passage *in extenso*, not only
because I am in full agreement with my late colleague's argument, but because it leads by easy
transition to the vexed question of the City Gates.
But before I plunge into the complexities of that
subject, I take opportunity to point out that there
is one old stage direction which appears to me to
yield substantiation to the Bradley-Archer theory
of the open-sided rear stage. In *1 Henry VI*, iii, 3,
the scene is the plains near Rouen. Charles, the
Bastard of Orleans, Alençon, and La Pucelle, with
soldiers, occupy the stage. Drums are heard afar
off. Then comes the direction, "Here sound [an

English march. Enter, and pass over at a distance, Talbot and his forces." Immediately afterwards the strains of a French march are heard, and the Duke of Burgundy and *his* forces enter and pass over in the same way. Personally, I cannot take "pass over at a distance" to mean anything otherwise than that the two armed bodies crossed over in succession from one side to the other of the rear stage.

I do not propose considering here all the hare-brained theories which have been advanced in futile attempts to solve the problem of the exact location of the device known as "the City Gates." [1] No one on this score has left himself more open to ridicule than Brodmeier, who asserts that the two regulation entering doors answered for the gates in *Coriolanus*. William Archer's unpublished comment on this will suffice:

Quite apart from other difficulties, Brodmeier's idea that the two frontal doors represented the gates is very absurd. Why should Corioli have gates at the space of a few feet from each other? Gates is evidently used of the two leaves of a single gateway.

Though arrived at independently, my own solution of the problem is practically identical with the solution propounded a decade ago by Miss Charlotte Porter, in the American-issued First Folio edition of Shakespeare, and more recently advocated by Mr.

[1] See G. P. Baker, *The Development of Shakespeare as a Dramatist*, p. 80; G. H. Cowling, *Music on the Shakespearean Stage*, p. 38; Crei-zenach, *The English Drama in the Age of Shakespeare*, p. 373.

R. Crompton Rhodes in his little book on *The Stagery of Shakespeare*.[1] It must not be assumed, however, that the matter is one of personal opinion: beyond the back of the rear stage, there is absolutely no other available place for the City Gates. But I fancy I hear someone protest: "Yes, but you have already demonstrated the existence of a door at the back of the rear stage, and a door surely implies a permanent wall. How, then, can you reconcile the two statements?" Well, it seems to me not improbable that the leaves of the gate formed the permanent background of the rear stage, and that in one of them there was a door through which, when the scene represented something otherwise than the outside of city walls, the characters came in and went out. At one time I was inclined to believe that this middle or back door really typified the city gates, — a by no means improbable idea, — but the evidence seems to me now to favor the more elaborate conception. There is reason to think that, when the gates were not forced in a general assault, it was the door rather than the gates that was opened. Consider for a moment some of the stage business in that undivided play, The *True Tragedie of Richard, Duke of Yorke*.[2] In this, Edward and Richard and their troupe of Hollanders

[1] Chap. 4.

[2] Reprinted in *Shakespeare's Library*, Hazlitt editor, 2d edit., vol. vi (see pp. 81, 82).

reach the gates of York only to find them closed. They sound up the drums. Direction: "Enter the Lord Maire of Yorke upon the wals." He agrees to open the gates "presentlie," and disappears. By the time Richard has delivered a speech of a poor ten words, the Mayor has descended below. Another direction says: "The Maire opens the dore and brings the kiee's in his hand." Why "door" here, unless there was a door in the gates?

In the one play it was sometimes the gates and sometimes the door that was employed. In Munday's *John a Kent and John a Cumber*, act III, Sir John Griffin, referring to John a Cumber's action, says, "And see, he sets the Castell gate wide ope." This was evidently a slow process, as an accompanying direction says, "Musique whyle he opens the door." But later on, after the four antiques have entered the castle, we have a direction, relative to John a Cumber, "Exit into the Castell and makes fast the dore." Subsequently, John a Kent says, "The gate fast my Lordes, etc." and an accompanying direction intimates that "he tryes the dore." It might of course be argued that *gate* and *door* are here interchangeable terms and referred to the gate only, but I have reasons for not accepting that view. In that mysterious old play, *Lady Alimony*,[1] we read in act III, scene 6, that a placard is placed on "the portal of a gate" that it might be readily ob-

[1] Reprinted in Hazlitt's edit. of Dodsley's *Old Plays*.

servable. What otherwise can this signify than that there was a door in the gate?

It must be admitted, of course, that there are sundry situations in old plays where the word "gate" is used purely in the sense of door; and it may well be that, where reference is made to the gates of mansions or private houses, a door was meant and perhaps one of the frontal doors used. Take for example *2 Henry IV*, 1, 2, as in the Quarto. "Enter the Lord Bardolfe at one doore." He asks, "who keepes the gate here ho? Where is the Earle?" and the porter replies:

> What shall I say you are? . . .
> His Lordship is walkt forth into the orchard,
> Please it your honour knocke but at the gate,
> And he himselfe will answer.

Then, "Enter the Earl Northumberland." Note here in the first case, that three separate entrances are used. Bardolfe, after coming on by the one frontal door, walks over to the other, knocks, and brings out the Porter. The gate through which Northumberland entered must have been the middle door, since it would have been highly absurd for him to open a pair of large gates for the purpose. But the porter's use of the term "gate" localizes the door, and practically shows that it was within a gate.[1]

[1] For other instances where gates otherwise than city gates are referred to, see *The Taming of the Shrew*, 1, 2; *The Silver Age* act II (where Amphitrio finds the gates of his house closed); *The Devil's Law*

Only one other bit of stage business that I know of indicates that the city gates were in a recess. In *The Faithful Friends*, III, 3, the scene being before the walls of the Sabine City, we have the direction: "They march together, and at the entrance of the gate Marius is stabbed."

One reason why I cannot agree that, in siege scenes and the like, the middle door of itself, without further division of the back wall, did duty for the gates, is that occasionally we find mention of "the Gates" (in the plural) being wrenched or forced upon. The clearest example is in *The Jewes Tragedy*, a Caroline play, in which, in act III, scene 2, we get the sequence, "It thunders and he wrenches the gate . . . thunders agen, he opens the gates." [1] In most siege scenes, the audience could hardly have been put off with a paltry make-believe, more especially in those scenes where the besieged first appear on the walls, otherwise the upper stage, and then come down and open the gates. Instances occur in *3 Henry VI*, IV, 7, *The Scottish Historie of James IV*, V, 3, and *Alphonsus, King of Arragon*, act V. In all such scenes, after being used at the outset for entry, the two frontal doors were suppressed by convention.

Case, II, 2 (bellman episode); *The English Traveller*, IV, 1; and *'Tis Pity She's A Whore*, III, scena ultima.

[1] Cf. *1 Henry VI*, I, 3, and III, 2; *The Silver Age*, Heywood's Works, ed. Pearson, III, p. 157; "They beate against the gates. Enter Cerberus."

A good deal of unnecessary mystery has been created by the fact that, besides the commoner scenes located in front of closed gates, a few scenes are now and again located behind them. At least one prominent investigator, Professor G. F. Reynolds, has expressed himself as perplexed on this score. Yet the explanation is simple. The one set of gates did duty for both kinds of scenes, the dialogue conveying to the audience on which side of the gates they were supposed to be. Examples of the reverse scene, where the gates are forced from the back or the characters come through them into an interior, occur in *I Henry VI*, III, 2, in the Porter scene in *Macbeth*, in the 1616 quarto of *Doctor Faustus*, where "the Clowns bounce at the gate within," and in *A New Way to Pay old Debts*, II, 2.[1]

If I were asked to say what are the most striking differences between the Elizabethan drama and the drama of the last generation or so, I should be careful to include in my categorical reply the frequency of balcony and window scenes in seventeenth-century drama as contrasted with their rarity in the drama of yesterday and to-day. In the uprise of the window-scene convention one sees the influence of the Italian Renaissance. If we cast our minds back to the days of ancient Rome, we shall find that Plautine and Terentian dramaturgy was an affair

[1] In the old quarto only. Here Gifford has tinkered with the stage directions.

of the open: the scene was the street. With the
rebirth of literature and art in Italy, and the frequent revival of the plays of Plautus and Terence,
the same fixed scene became the model, but the
neo-classic dramatists wore their rue with a difference. Windows were not brought into play in the
old Roman drama because the windows of ancient
Rome were placed at too high an elevation to be
pressed into service in the traffic of the stage. But
in fifteenth-century Italy this drawback did not
exist, the result being that the neo-classic dramatist,
foreseeing their efficacy, made telling use of window
scenes. As one finds clearly demonstrated in *Ralph
Roister Doister*, and *Mother Bombie*, English play-
wrights, in basing on the Plautine or Terentian
scheme, also took stock of the new Italian extension,
thus establishing insularly a convention which the
inn-yard playing-places were readily capable of
fostering, and which they did so far foster that the
window scene grew to be an important integrant of
Elizabethan dramaturgy.[1] These facts have never
yet been fully recognized. They had not swum into
my ken when I wrote the section on "Windows in
the Elizabethan Theatre," reprinted from *Anglia*
in the Second Series of my *Elizabethan Playhouse*,
the first study of the subject ever made. Since this

[1] See Gascoigne's *The Supposes*, a play of Italian origin acted at
Gray's Inn in 1566, for the employment of windows in a unified Serlio
setting. For windows in academic plays (*e.g.* *Susenbrotus*, at Cambridge, in 1615), see the Shakespeare *Jahrbuch* for 1911, p. 77.

is readily accessible to most students, I need not go twice over ground already well traversed. Further research, however, on my part during the past decade has brought to light some valuable new data warranting comment on one or two points already discussed. Moreover, I have discovered evidence of the existence of a stage feature hitherto unsuspected, to wit, a grated opening on the ground floor of the tiring-house. This was probably situated at a height of about five feet between the rear-stage curtains and one of the entering doors: a breaking-up of the intermediate space which goes to indicate the absurdity of supposing that any hangings could have been placed there. Its existence is clearly proved, I think, by a stage direction in Marston's *Antonio's Revenge*, II, 3;[1] but, lest I be reminded that one swallow does not make a summer, it seems advisable to cite other examples. Act V, scene 2, of *Eastward Hoe* is a prison scene. Holdfast and Bramble enter. Bramble wishes to speak to Security, one of the prisoners, and Security hails him. Definite stage directions are lacking, but Security evidently appears at the grated opening to which he makes reference. He says: "My case, Master Bramble, is stone walls and iron grates; you see it, this is the weakest part on 't. And for getting me forth, no means but hang myself, and so be carried

[1] Malone Society reprint, line 844; "Antonio kisseth Mellida's hand: then Mellida goes from the grate."

forth, from which they have bound me in intolerable bands." Security, being bound, could not walk on. Toward the end of the act, he again calls out without entering, no doubt showing himself once more at the grate to sing his lament. Afterwards, Touchstone says, "Bring him forth, Master Wolf, and release his bands." Unless one here assumes the existence of a grate a little above stage level, it is impossible to visualize the action.

Again, in Fletcher's *The Woman's Prize*, III, 4, we have clear proof of a small opening near one of the entrance doors. The scene is a hall in Petruchio's house. Petruchio has been pretending illness or madness, and the house is in a state of upset. Maria calls in the watch and has all the doors locked. Petruchio is heard storming off the stage, and he finally bawls out:

> If any man misdoubt me for infected,
> There is mine arm, let any man look on 't!

Saying this, he thrusts his arm through an opening, and the Doctor comes on and feels his pulse. Subsequently, Petruchio, after demanding his release in no half-hearted way, according to the stage direction, "bursts the door open, and enters with a fowling piece."

Compare the action in act IV, scene 4 of *The Humorous Lieutenant*. Here the Lieutenant stands in dread uncertainty outside Demetrius's apartment, not knowing exactly what stern preparation has been made for the reception of unwelcome visitors. He is dared to go to the door, and first knocks at it gently, then saying,

> stay, stay:
> Here is a window; I will see, stand wide.
> By heaven, he's charging of a gun!

Then, he knocks again at the door but more loudly than before, peeps again through the window, and finally provokes Demetrius into coming forth, pistol in hand. The eighth scene of the same act evidently passes in the same place. Celia enters with some others. She "knocks at the window" and calls to her distraught lover, but meeting with no response, remonstrates with

> Can you be drowsy
> When I call at your window?

I am now forced to consider what bearing my recent conclusion to the effect that the fixture known as the city gates had a door in one of its leaves has on my earlier conclusion, as arrived at in my study of Stage Windows in *The Elizabethan Playhouse*, second series,[1] that the rear stage had a window for theatrical purposes at its back. Many situations in old plays, some of them presently to be discussed, point to the existence of this window. Yet, on first thoughts, the presence of such a feature in a city gate seems more than a trifle incongruous,

---

[1] Pp. 50 *et seq.*

and one is tempted to take the window as imaginary. But what we have once more to bear in mind is that no permanent appurtenance of the Elizabethan stage had existence in the eyes of the audience until it was actually pressed into the service of the scene. The rear stage was used mostly to represent a room, and to begin boggling over the window would be to end by objecting that a pair of large gates hardly formed a fitting background for a room. It may be that, when not required by the action, the window was obscured in some way; but it was certainly not imaginary. Nothing was imagined on the Elizabethan stage that could conveniently be shown.

To the instances cited in my earlier study of situations calling for the presence of a rear-stage window some further examples may be added. If we examine both the Quarto and the Folio text of *Richard III*, we shall find that in act III, scene 5, where Richard and Buckingham come on in ill-favored armor, there is nothing to show that they enter elsewhere than on the lower stage. It is their cue to pretend alarm in the presence of the Lord Mayor. Richard warns them to "look to the draw-bridge there"; Buckingham hears, or pretends to hear, a drum, and then the Crookback commands Catesby to "Ore-looke the walls." Writing of this scene in an unpublished note, William Archer says: "This might seem like an instance of outlook from the stage; but it is pretty clear that if Catesby even pretended to carry out the injunction, he left the stage to so do."

But, it needs to be pointed out, in opposition to that view, that we have no record of Catesby's exit. Compare *The Widow*, III, 4, where the scene is laid in Brandino's House. After the disguised Martia's exit to take horse, Violetta watches "his" departure, either through a window on stage level or through a door. She comments upon the speed with which "he" gallops off, and later, when her mistress is anxious that "he" should be called back, says it is too late, he being then out of sight. It is interesting to note that there is an analogous situation in the fourth act of *The Alchemist*, more particularly as *The Widow* was written in collaboration and Jonson was one of its authors. Moreover, the two plays, to my mind, belong to very much the same period. It would be difficult, however, to light upon a decade in the first half of the seventeenth century in which illustration of the use of this rear-stage window does not occur. Look, for example, at act II, scene 3 of that late Jacobean play, *The Humorous Lieutenant*. This may be taken as a disclosed scene, since Leucippe is found reading with her two maids sitting at a table writing. A knock within causes Leucippe to ask, "Who's that? Look out! to your business, maid!" Evidently the maid addressed looks out of a window, as she at once replies that the caller is "an ancient woman, with a maid attending"; and the two referred to then enter.

Then we proceed along to Caroline times, and pause before Brome's *The New Academy, or the New Exchange*. From this, I quote without comment a slice from act IV, scene 2, an interior:

Enter Hannah, Cash.

HAN. The Ladies man's without: who came to know if the house were ready to entertain 'hem; do you know 'em, Mr. Lightfoot?

STRI. I have heard o' th' lady. Cash, see if it be Ephraim. He cannot know thee. Let him not away.

He looks out.

CASH. 'T is he, I see him hither.

One other feature of the ground floor of the tiring-house remains to be discussed before we make our way upstairs and leave it for good. We know from sundry old plays that some sort of architectural projection was called "the penthouse," and, difficult as is the task, it is our business to discover exactly what it was. "Penthouse" is commonly defined nowadays as "a shed standing aslope from a main building"; but Mr. J. Alfred Gotch, in treating of Elizabethan architecture in *Shakespeare's England*,[1] writes of the houses in the smaller towns: "From the front wall of the house there often projected, on the level of the first floor, a sloping

[1] II, p. 63.

tiled ledge, called the penthouse; on the ground beneath there stood a stall, which served as shopcounter when the householder was engaged in retail trade."

It is noteworthy also that Cotgrave, in his French-English Dictionary, defines *soupendüe* as "a penthouse; iuttie or part of a building that iutteth beyond or leaneth ouer the rest." Having now acquired a fair idea of what a stage penthouse really was, let us look at one or two situations in the old drama where it is either referred to or utilized. In *The Merchant of Venice*, II, 6, Gratiano says: "This is the penthouse under which Lorenzo desired us to make stand"; and in *Much ado about Nothing*, III, 3, ll. 110–112, we find Borachio giving the order, "Stand thee close vnder this penthouse, for it drizzels rain, and I will, like a true drunkard, vtter all to thee." A much later instance is to be found in Davenant's *The Distresses*, II, I, where the musicians come on to accompany a serenade. Says the First Musician:

> Stand all close beneath,
> The penthouse! There's a certain chambermaid,
> From yond casement, will dash us else.[1]

---

[1] "Under this Tarias," in *Every Man Out of his Humour*, II, I, l. 1001 (Malone Society reprint) would seem to imply the penthouse. The same architectural feature was demanded by the situation in *The Woman Hater*, IV, 2, a street scene, where Oriana and her woman appear at a window, and Gondarius, in entering with the duke, Valdre, and Arrigo, espies her, and bids the others hide while he engages her

These references are of such a nature that the penthouse could not have been imaginary: as a matter of fact we have a faint clue to the manner in which it was constructed. There are certain stipulations in the Fortune contract which recall Cotgrave's description of *soupendüe* as "a penthouse iuttie or part of a building that iutteth beyond or leaneth ouer the rest." We learn in that contract that each of the two upper galleries which went around the three sides and part of the fourth side of the building had a successive jutty forward of some ten inches. As the tiring-house front was part of the circulating architectural disposition of the interior, it is rational to assume that each of its two stories, in correspondence with the two upper galleries of the auditorium, had a like, though perhaps not the same, series of jutties. We find a narrow sloping projection of this order depicted in the Messalina engraving;[1] but, since the curtains are depicted as hanging from the front of this, it could hardly have represented, at all junctures, the penthouse under which the characters realistically took

in conversation. Valdre says, "Here we shall stand unseen, and near enough."

Neuendorff, *Die englische Volksbühne im Zeitalter Shakespeares*, p. 89, ties himself into a hopeless knot in discussing the penthouse, and is seemingly inclined to identify it with the shed mentioned in Henslowe's Diary as being attached to the Rose!

[1] See the enlargement in A. Nicoll, *British Drama*, p. 70.

shelter from the harsh elements and unsympathetic chambermaids. Hence, I am compelled to assume that the base of the gallery which ran along the front of the tiring-house on first story-level did duty for the penthouse.

As for the associated problem of "the bulk," what it was and where it was situated, I confess myself unable to make attempt at a solution. It was probably no more imaginary than the penthouse. In *Othello*, v, 1, Iago says at the opening of the scene, to Roderigo, "Here, stand behind this bulk; straight will he come. Wear thy good rapier here, and put it home." All I know is that a bulk was some kind of projection from a house, but knowing that, I am none the wiser.

It is unfortunate that the precise arrangement of the first story of the tiring-house, the relativity of its parts, is not so well assured as the disposition of its ground floor, since it too had vital, though not so frequent, association with the action. One or two boxes were provided here for certain favored spectators; but what is really important for us to note is that, as already stated in part, a balustraded gallery ran along its front, and that it had centrally a curtained room corresponding with, but a trifle smaller than, the rear stage. This section of the tiring-house was generally referred to in stage directions, somewhat vaguely, as "above" or "aloft," but it was also known and sometimes textually spoken of as "the upper stage." [1]

The prototype of the public-theatre gallery was the lower gallery of the old inn-yards — one reason among several why it may be assumed to have extended right across the tiring-house. That it was certainly of no brevity is demonstrated by the action in *1 Henry VI*, II, I, where Talbot, Bedford, and Burgundy ascend by scaling ladders at three different places, to start a fight which ends in the French leaping over the walls in their shirts. This is a typical example of the great utility of the gallery in siege scenes; but my main reason for singling it out for citation is that it affords apt illustration of the not uncommon action of characters jumping down onto the stage — a perilous feat if the gallery had been situated at any particular height.[2] But it must be remembered that the

[1] In Marston's *Antonio and Mellida*, I, I, l. 341, the existence of the term "upper stage" is implied in the direction beginning, "Exeunt all on the lower stage." See also Day's *Humour out of Breath*, IV, 3, for stage directions mentioning both the upper and the lower stages. A textual reference to both stages, in a passage dealing with a recent Samson play, is likewise to be found in Middleton's *The Family of Love*, I, 3 (cf. Chambers, *The Eliz. Stage*, III, 120).

[2] If, as I take it, the front of the lowermost gallery in the public theatre was on stage level, and the front of the middle gallery on upper-stage level, then the height of the balcony in the Fortune was twelve feet. According to the measurements of the Hope, the same height applied in that house. As the Hope was modelled on the Swan, and the Fortune on the Globe, it appears to me that the galleries of the auditorium and the stories of the tiring-house were of the same relative heights in all.

Elizabethan players were nothing if not acrobats. It is permissible to deduce from the Fortune contract that the gallery of that house was twelve feet from the stage, a height from which it must have been difficult for little Prince Arthur to jump to his death without breaking any of his bones.[1] But to assume this to have been the normal elevation of the gallery in public and private theatres alike is to be confronted with divers difficulties. There is, for example, a situation in Massinger's *The Picture*, a Globe and Blackfriars play of the Caroline period, which proves not a little puzzling. In act IV, scene 2, a trick is played on Ubaldo and Ricardo. They are imprisoned in two contiguous upper chambers, and show themselves at windows or grates. But their position cannot be one of any particular elevation, seeing that Sophia instructs the servants who are on the lower stage to reach them up certain things to work with.

In early dramatic literature, the gallery is to be found masquerading under a variety of names. That part of it which fronted the upper curtained space was known as the balcony, and it was there that Juliet leaned over and drank in Romeo's honied words.[2] What it was called at any particular juncture depended much on the synchronal action:

[1] Cf. *Fortune by Land and Sea*, III, 1, where Forrest leaps down.

[2] In Brome's Caroline comedy, *The Weeding of Covent Garden; or The Middlesex Justice of Peace*, comes the early direction, "Enter Dorcas above upon a Bellconie, Gabriel gazes at her."

sometimes it was referred to as "the walls," and
sometimes as "the terrace." [1]

We have seen that there were three modes of entrance to the lower stage, two by frontal doors and
one through the curtains (or the door behind them).
There is good reason to believe that a similar number of entrances, similarly disposed, gave onto the
gallery. Entrance through the curtains of the upper
room needs no proving: what one is required to
prove is the existence of a door at either end of the
gallery. There is not an abundance of evidence on
the point, but what we have suffices. Those of my
readers who are well read in the Elizabethan Drama
will recall that some years ago the Malone Society
reprinted the anonymous tragedy of *The Life and
Death of Claudius Tiberius Nero*, originally issued
in 1607. Written by some university scholar, this
play, in all probability, was never acted, but the
author shows his acquaintanceship with stage
technicalities, and his stage directions are phrased
and framed in the orthodox theatrical style. Thus,
at line 1598, we have: "Enter Caligula at one end of
the stage and Sejanus at the other end below. Iulia
at one end aloft, and Tiberius at the other."

This goes far, I think, to prove the two upper-
stage doors. Of equal clearness is the situation in

---

[1] Cf. *2 Henry VI* (First Folio, p. 142): "Enter King, Queene and
Somerset on the Tarras." Also *Every Man Out*, II, 1, line 1001 (Malone Society reprint).

Heywood's *The Rape of Lucrece*, v, 3. Here the evidence is from a Red Bull play of the early Jacobean period. Horatius is standing in defence of the bridge across the Tiber. His position, most likely, is near one of the normal entering doors. As Tarquin and the rest enter, there is, says the stage direction, "a noise of knocking down the bridge within," and then "enter in severall places, Sextus and Valerius above." They are supposed to call from opposite hills, Sextus reproaching Tarquin and Valerius threatening Horatius. When the bridge falls, Horatius disappears as if into the Tiber, and Sextus describes his amazing progress:

> Lo! he swims armed as he is,
> Whilst all the army have discharged their arrows,
> Of which the shield upon his back is full, etc.

The bridge, the Tiber, and the swimming had all to be imagined. These were among the things that the Elizabethan stage could *not* show.

It is noteworthy, furthermore, that there are several old plays whose action calls occasionally for the use of a single upper-stage door. No particular stress can be laid, however, on *Titus Andronicus*, v, 2, because the "business" here is doubtful. We are told that Titus makes his appearance by opening his "study Dore," and we find that he is aloft, because he is at once asked to come down; but we cannot be certain that he really opens a door. His emergence through the upper-stage curtains would answer equally as well — perhaps, indeed, better, because the position, being central, would have been more advantageous for the general sight. On the whole, we are, I think, on safer ground in dealing with the situation in the anonymous undivided play, *A Knacke to Know a Knave*, which seems to demand the use of an upper-stage door. At a certain juncture it is conveyed to the audience that Orphinio and Zepherius have been locked up in a loft. At line 1670, in the Malone Society reprint, we get the direction, "Enter Phillida with the keyes to release them," Phillida evidently coming on above, though the point is not assured. After indulging in a soliloquy, she opens the door and releases the two brethren. They are still within the castle, and she gives them a signet to show to the porter, so that they may not be stopped at the gate.

Just one word more on this score, by way of warning. The fact must not be overlooked that characters had other means of appearing above besides coming on through doors or curtains, or being disclosed on the upper stage. A stage direction in that highly mysterious old play *Lady Alimony* contributes to our knowledge in this respect. In act IV, scene 6, we read at the opening that "The Favourites appear to their half bodies in their shirts, in rooms above." These rooms, and the curtained space which separated them, are plainly to be seen in Kirkman's well-known view of the Red Bull stage.

Those of my readers who happen to have studied my paper on early theatrical music, reprinted in *The Elizabethan Playhouse*, First Series, may possibly recall that, considerably over a decade ago, I saw reason to propound a theory concerning the curtained upper room which postulated for it a tripartite utility. Though, broadly speaking, it was practically a duplication of the rear stage, it was much less frequently pressed into service for dramatic purposes; and it was the rarity of its employment as a factor of stage illusion, combined with sundry items of suggestive evidence, which eventually forced me to conclude that, besides its dramatic use, it had one or two other offices. The sad fact remains that my early theory, that the curtained upper room had secondary employment as a general dressing room and as the normal place for the performance of incidental music, has by no means met with unanimous acceptance. Sir Edmund Chambers and Professor G. F. Reynolds have both entered demurrers.[1] Hitherto I have had no opportunity of making reply on this score, and the present seems to me a fitting moment to rediscuss the question.

Generally speaking, in early days most of the dressing for the performance of a play took place

---

[1] Chambers, *The Eliz. Stage*, ii, 542 (especially note 4); iii, 119, 120. See also Professor Reynolds's paper, "Another Principle of Elizabethan Staging," in *The Manly Anniversary Studies in Language and Literature*, p. 76.

before the play began; and no cogent reason can be advanced why, during the period while the audience was slowly assembling, the curtained upper room should not have been used as a dressing-room. The action of the play rarely, if ever, began there: I am wholly at a loss to recall an example. Then again, my assumption that the room was also used as a music room in no wise runs counter to the theory that it served as a dressing-room. Of course, I am speaking now purely of the public theatre: in the private houses there were special customs which would probably have prevented the use of the room as a dressing-room. We know that in the second Blackfriars, early in its history, both vocal and instrumental music was given before the play and also in the intervals.[1] But it cannot be proved that in the public theatres anything of the nature of an overture was ever provided; and it is not even certain that inter-act music was performed there before the later Caroline period.[2] At present, however,

[1] C. W. Wallace, *The Children of the Chapel at Blackfriars*, pp. 105–107; W. J. Lawrence on "Music in the Elizabethan Theatre," in *The Musical Quarterly*, VI, no. 2 (1920), pp. 192 ff.

[2] Gayton, in his *Art of Longevity* (1659), avers that hazel-nuts and filberts are very indigestible:

> "Yet upon these the vulgar sort do feed.
> As at the Playhouses, betwixt the Acts,
> The Musick Room is drown'd with these nut-cracks."

From this, and Braithwaite's allusion to "the encurtained musick" playing in the intervals, it is fairly assured that entr'acte music was regularly given in all kinds of theatres in Caroline times.

I am not much concerned to establish the use of the curtained upper room as a dressing-room, the point not being really vital. What I am concerned to demonstrate is that the room was the normal habitat of the musicians — a thing that matters — and on that score I shall fight, if need be, on my stumps.

Sir Edmund Chambers expresses grave doubts about the fundamentibility of the theatre music-room, and is inclined to believe that the theatre had been an organized institution for thirty years before the musicians occupied any regular place.[1] But he does not show proof of having done any very solid thinking about the matter. The possibilities of precedent are wholly ignored. It would surely have given him pause had he recalled how long before the Elizabethan period it had been customary, not in England alone but in Europe generally, to give the musicians, when playing either publicly or privately before large assemblies, an elevated position. From an acoustic standpoint there was sound sense in this: it ensured a full and proper conveyance of the music.[2] But Chambers is not

---

[1] *The Eliz. Stage*, ii, 542.

[2] Cf. the views in Gaston Vuillier, *A History of Dancing* (1898), pp. 68, 83; also the plate of the French court ballet of 1635 in Germain Bapst, *Essai sur L'Histoire de Théâtre*, p. 217. For early Italian court-theatre procedure, see W. J. Lawrence on "The English Theatre Orchestra: its Rise and Early Characteristics," in *The Musical Quarterly*, III, no. 1 (1917), p. 11.

alone in his superficial thinking about this matter. It does not seem to have struck any of our musico-dramatic historians that the prototype of the early theatrical music room was the music gallery of the old banqueting halls, or that there is high probability that in that notable precursor of the theatre, the inn-yard playing place, the musicians took their stand over the stage on one of the permanent galleries of the yard.

We are so habituated nowadays to see the fiddlers in their distracting position below the stage that we are apt to look upon any other place for them as outrageous, forgetful of a fact that Pepys long ago noted, that the orchestral box is the worst possible contrivance for the transmission of music — and equally ignoring that the English theatre had been institutionalized for well-nigh a century before the principle now obtaining was adopted. The orchestral box is an offshoot of opera, not of drama. It owed its creation to the necessity of a close association between instruments and voice; the same necessity which, at an earlier period, brought the Elizabethan lutanist onto the stage to accompany the dramatic singer.

Let us now consider Chambers's pronouncements on the subject. He writes, on first broaching it:

A special music room perhaps existed already in the Swan in 1611, and, if so, may have been, as it was in the later theatres, in the upper part of the tire-house.

A footnote to this adds:

Chaste Maid in Cheapside, v, 4 (s. d.): "There is a sad song in the music-room." Cf. *Thracian Wonder*, iv, 1, 182; "Pythias speaks in the musick Room behind the Curtain," 186, "Pythia above, behind the curtains." But these, although early plays, are in late prints, and the other examples of a music room "above" given by Lawrence, i, 91, are Caroline. Jasper Mayne says of Jonson (1638, *Jonsonus Virbius*), "Thou laidst no sieges to the music-room."

I interrupt here to give a fuller quotation from Mayne, in order to show what he was driving at. In the midst of a long elegy, he writes:

Thy scene was free from monsters; no hard plot
Call'd down a God t'untie th' unlikely knot;
The stage was still a stage, two entrances
Were not two parts o' the world, disjoin'd by seas.
Thine were land-tragedies no prince was found
To swim a whole scene out then o' the stage drown'd;
Pitch'd fields, as Red-bull wars, still felt thy doom;
Thou laid'st no sieges to the music room.[1]

What Mayne implies by this last line is that Jonson had no scaling scenes in his plays, such as were common features of the Chronicle Histories.[2]

Chambers, continuing, says:

My own impression is that when the lord's room over the tire-house was disused by spectators (cf. p. 537), it became

---

[1] Bradley and Adams, *The Jonson Allusion Book*, p. 227.

[2] Echoed by Wilson in his prologue to *The Cheats*, wherein it is said that the coming play has "no tedious sieges to the Musick-Room." This piece was produced at the Vere Street Theatre in March, 1663, and the reference helps to establish the fact that that theatre was fitted up in the old platform-stage style.

indifferently available for actors and for music, and that here, rather than, as is possible, higher still in the scenic wall, was the normal place for the seventeenth-century music, when it was not needed elsewhere, or the space needed for other purposes.

In proceeding to examine this statement of opinion, we may, in the first case, dismiss from our minds the alleged possibility of a music-room higher than the first story of the tiring-house. It is wholly against the evidence. Nor must the Lords' room be in anywise confused with the curtained upper stage beside which it stood: what we have to bear in mind is that there was only one curtained space aloft. Happily, I am absolved from the necessity of discussing the position and history of the Lords' room by the circumstance that I have already devoted a section to the subject in my first book on *The Elizabethan Playhouse*. But it is vital to observe that Chambers, in stating that the room was eventually disused by spectators, misreads his authority. He is making deductions from a well-known paragraph in the sixth chapter of Dekker's *The Guls Horn-booke*, that immortal piece of irony, which, although not published until 1609, bears evidence, both in its address to the reader and in its topical allusions, to the as yet unrecognized fact that it had been written some five or six years previously. Its references apply more to 1603 than to 1609. Now, Dekker does not say that the Lords' room had been disused by spectators; what he does imply is that it had been abandoned by its original frequenters and adopted as a rendezvous by waiting-women and gentlemen ushers. So far from there being any material disuse of the first story of the tiring-house by spectators in the first half of the seventeenth century, the evidence is to the contrary. All the views of playhouse interiors, from the Dutch sketch of the Swan to Kirkman's plate of the Red Bull in Commonwealth times, with the exception of the *Messalina* view, show the presence of spectators in boxes immediately above the stage. Accordingly, we have no reason to assume that the musicians waited until the complete abandonment of the Lords' room before taking up their position on the first story of the tiring-house.

My own opinion is that the provision of a music room, so far from being a seventeenth-century afterthought, dated from the actual inception of the theatre. It appears to me that, to establish that point, all one requires to do is to demonstrate that hidden instrumental music was a theatrical characteristic from the earliest period, and that the first public theatres possessed a curtained upper room. From sundry stage directions in late sixteenth-century plays, we know that it was customary then to intensify the emotion evoked by pathetic situations by strains of music from an unseen source. An example is to be found in the vision scene in the third act of Greene's *Alphonsus, King of Arragon*, a play supposed to date from about 1587, though not printed until twelve years later. Another is to hand in Heywood's anonymously issued *Edward IV, Part II*, which was entered on the Stationers' register on August 28, 1599, as acted by Derby's Men. In this there is a touching scene in the Tower, where the two little princes kneel down in silent prayer at their bedside, and remain motionless for a time while solemn music is heard.[1] So, too, in Dekker's *Old Fortunatus*, there are certain speeches in the third act which had a running musical accompaniment, a device not wholly unknown in our own day.[2] And should we not be within our rights to assume that, with realistic appropriateness, the musicians were in their gallery in that well-remembered scene in *Twelfth Night*, where, in response to the love-sick Duke's command, they send forth the strains of "the old and antic song" just before Feste comes on to sing it? I shall be told, of course, that this is a flagrant begging of the question. It will be urged that I have not yet demonstrated the sixteenth-century existence of an upper curtained room, or advanced proof that the sixteenth-century musicians occupied an elevated position. Well, as for the latter objection, it can be answered, I think, by citing a stage direction from Whetstone's *Promos and Cassandra, Part II*, act I, scene 9: "Five or

[1] Heywood's Works, edit. Pearson (1874), i, 153, 154.
[2] For a later example, see *The Captain*, IV, 5.

sixe, the one half men, the other women, near vnto the musick, singing on some stage, erected from the ground: During the first parte of the song, the King faineth to talke sadlie, with some of his Counsell."

It is true that this play was printed in 1578, but two years after the first public theatre was opened, and that we have no record that it was ever acted; but it remains to be noted that the direction just cited takes it for granted that the musicians will occupy an elevated position. If one could only demonstrate the existence of an upper curtained room in the playhouse somewhere about that period, the point might be looked upon as proved; but that is precisely what one cannot do. Evidence establishing the upper curtained room is not to be found before the Jacobean period, but certain earlier situations seem to point to its previous existence. One of these occurs in *2 Henry IV*, iv, 5, where there is textual indication that music is played "off" to soothe the sick king, though the stage direction is missing. "Call for the music in the other room," surely means that the music was to play somewhere behind curtains, either on the rear or the upper stage. Again, there is a scene in Munday's *Death of Robert, Earl of Huntington*, v, 2, already discussed by me in my section on Windows in *The Elizabethan Playhouse*, Second Series,[1] which seems to demand the use of a curtained upper room.

[1] Second Series, p. 34

With the dawn of the seventeenth century the evidence gets a trifle clearer, but it is mostly private-theatre evidence. There are textual indications in *The Malcontent* that the discordant music heard at the opening was played above. This was a Black-friars play of *circa* 1602 and a Globe play of 1604. *The Fawne* of the same author came intermediately. It seems fairly well assured that in the fifth act of this play a curtain was drawn when Tiberio and Dulcimel are disclosed standing hand and hand above. Moreover, the use of an upper chamber is indicated in *The Miseries of Enforced Marriage*, a Globe play of 1605, though no mention of curtains is made in connection with it. For positive proof of the upper curtains we have to rely upon later evidence, such as the direction in *Henry VIII*, v, 2, and the silent testimony of the *Messalina* and the Red Bull prints.

It might, of course, be sensibly argued that the playing of incidental music off the stage does not necessarily imply an elevated position for the musician,[1] and, in face of that objection, I am forced to seek proof of their elevated position in other

[1] Not all music played by unseen executants was played in the tiring-house. Supernatural, and even pseudo-supernatural strains came either from beneath the stage or from "divers places." See *The Prophetess*, v, 3, and *Women Pleased*, v, 2. But where we get directions for "soft music" without indication of the visible presence of the musicians, it may be taken, I think, that the music was rendered in the elevated music room.

ways. The earliest and soundest evidence we have, I think, on the point lies in stage directions indicating the rendering of songs within the tiring-house. The boy who sang and the musicians who accompanied him all used the one music sheet on the one double-faced stand; and a few early directions show that the room occupied was not on stage level. Thus, in Marston's *The Wonder of Women, or Sophonisba*, a Blackfriars play of 1605, there is an instruction in the fourth act for "a short song to soft musick above." It may be objected that this was a private-theatre play, but similar intimations are soon afterwards to be found in public-theatre plays. To begin with, we have the instance cited by Chambers from *A Chaste Maid in Cheapside*, a Swan production of 1611, "There is a sad song in the music room"; about the first mention we get, I think, of the music room. That the Globe of the same period had a similar room, and that it was situated above, is shown by a textual reference in Beaumont and Fletcher's *The Captain*. In act III, scene 4, just before music is heard and the song, "Away delights" sung, Leila says to her maid:

> bid the boy go sing
> That song above, I gave him:
> The sad song.

So too, in *The Virgin Martyr*, a Red Bull play of 1622, occurs the prompter's marginal warning, "Rise, consort," signifying that the musicians are to be told to take their place above. Act v, scene 1, is a rear-stage scene representing Theophilus's study. The warning was for the soft music heard just as Angelo enters carrying the basket of fruit and flowers.

It is to be clearly deduced from one or two later plays that the music room was situated at an elevation, that it was fronted by curtains, and that it was occasionally used as a place of dramatic action. If this is not sufficient proof of its precise locality, if it fails to identify it with the curtained upper stage, I despair of ever winning acceptance for the best substantiated of theories. It is satisfactory to me to find that the evidence from *The Thracian Wonder*, long ago advanced by me in a study of "Music and Song in the Elizabethan Theatre,"[1] is amply corroborated by sundry details vouchsafed by a couple of late Caroline plays. In 1657, there was printed in octavo an anonymous, unacted tragi-comedy called *The False Favorite Disgrac'd, and The Reward of Loyalty*, which has been attributed to Balthazar Gerbier.[2] The author, whoever he may have been, evinces a thorough acquaintanceship with the prime characteristics of the old platform stage. In act III, toward the end, at what appears to be the opening of a scene, we have the direction: "Rosa[nia]

---

[1] *The Elizabethan Playhouse and Other Studies*, i, 91, 92.

[2] For whom see Dr. Hotson's Harvard thesis on "Sir William Davenant and the Commonwealth Drama."

and Dranetta in the Musique Room." Rosania begins by saying, "from this balcone, we shall behold all passages."

Let us turn now to Thomas Jordan's comedy, *Money is an Ass*, which was licensed for printing on November 16, 1667, and published in 1668, with the title-page notification, "as it hath been acted with good applause." This play has a cryptic prologue intimating that it had been written for a small company of eight players, evidently before the Civil War, as the directions are distinctly of the platform-stage order. But it is noteworthy that there is extant an unique variant of the piece, with the title altered to *Wealth Outwitted, or Money's an Ass*, and the substitution of a rhymed dedication to John Philips, Esq., for the leaf containing the prologue and the actors' names.[1] The opening lines of the dedication indicate that the play was not of recent date:

> This Play was writ by *Me*, & pleas'd the Stage,
> When I was not full fifteen years of age.

Unfortunately, we have no means of determining the year of Jordan's birth, but he started life as a boy-player and had come to maturity in 1640, or thereabouts. Of the players mentioned in the cast, Sands, Lovell, Loveday, and Jordan himself were all at Norwich with a large, hastily gathered com-

[1] See "G. T–D's" note on the subject in *The Review of English Studies*, i, 219.

pany in March, 1635; [1] and I am inclined to believe
that the play had been written a few years earlier.
In act IV, scene 1, we get the note, "Calumney
above" — evidently a prompter's warning, as
Calumney is not seen until later, his appearance
being indicated by the direction "Enter Callamney
in the Musique Room." He sneaks in then to
listen to what is being said below, and calls for his
master.　After the call, we have "Enter Clutch
above."

We thus see that there is valid evidence warranting the belief that from early Jacobean times onward, the curtained upper room was used in part
as a music room and in part as an acting-place; and
I also think we have reasonable grounds for supposing that this curtained upper room had been in existence from the earliest theatrical period.

The disposition and offices of the second story of
the tiring-house form, I fear, an unsolvable mystery.
I have an idea, born of sundry references in Henslowe's Diary and elsewhere, that some considerable
portion of this floor was devoted to the storing of
costumes, wigs, and light properties. [2] Undoubtedly,

---

[1] Cf. J. T. Murray, *English Theatrical Companies*, i, 279, 280. The
surmise that the company was that of the King's Revels is unwar-
ranted.

[2] Cf. Collier, *Annals of the Stage* (1831), iii, 356 *n.*, and 360. Brome
speaks of an "upper wardrobe" in Caroline times. See also Halliwell-
Phillipps, *Outlines of the Life of Shakespeare*, 4th edit. (1884), p. 360,
for ballad on the burning of the Globe, indicating that wigs and drum-

all the heavier properties would have been housed on stage level. There is a prevalent fallacy, to which even the normally cautious Chambers has sub- scribed,[1] that royal thrones were lowered from above in full sight of the audience, much as goods are low- ered in a warehouse — a rank misconception due to an unfortunate misreading of an old stage phrase which so frequently recurs in early stage directions. The blunder becomes apparent when it is pointed out that the technical term for the royal throne in Elizabethan days was "the state," and that the term "throne" was applied only to the chair in which divinities descended. One could concede that "the state" was thus lowered only on finding that other heavy properties were placed *in situ* in a similar way; but so far from this being the case, there is an abundance of evidence to prove that cur- tained beds and executioners' scaffolds were in- variably thrust out from the rear stage.

It is noteworthy that the tiring-house, considered as an entity, extended some five or six feet above the surrounding walls of the roofed galleries. In other words, a curious sort of garret surmounted the second story. Emerging from this garret was a pole on which, an hour or so before the performance, the symbolic flag of the theatre was hoisted, to

heads were stored above. The drum-heads were apparently used for simulating storms and were doubtless stored in the garret.

[1] *The Eliz. Stage*, iii, 77.

notify the public across the river that that was an acting-day. Through a window or door in the garret there were also given three trumpet-blasts at customary intervals, by way of final warning to intending playgoers. Both the flag and the trumpeter are to be seen in the well-known Dutch sketch of the Swan. Many references to both practices occur in Elizabethan literature. Middleton is prone to the making of metaphors based on the custom of the flag. Two of them are to be found in his *A Mad World, My Masters*, a play belonging to about 1608. In act III, scene 3, Follywit says of a certain person, "the hair about the hat is as good as a flag upo' the pole, at a common playhouse, to waft company"; a quaint simile from which one may draw the inference that flags were not hoisted on private theatres. Later on in the same play, we get, "'T is Lent in your cheeks: the flag is downe," — an allusion to the circumstance that plays were not given during the annual penitential period. So, too, in act IV, scene 2 of *The Roaring Girl*, Openwork, addressing the masked women, says, "Pray, tell me why your two flags were advanced; the comedy come, what's the comedy?" Note also the two following extracts from an anonymous elegy on Richard Burbage, the famous Globe actor, who died in the Lent of 1619:[1]

---

[1] Preserved in Sloane MSS, 1786, and printed by Mrs. Stopes in her paper on "The Burbages," in *Transactions of the Royal Society of Literature*, 1913, p. 145.

tectum

porticus

mimorum
ædes

orchestra

sedilia

ingressus

proscænium

planities siue arena

humum sed disci et serendum, histracum confectub[oni]
ni destinatum, in quo multi vrsi, tauri, et stupenda
magnitudinis canes, distentis caueis et septis aluntur; qui
ad

And you, his sad companions, to whom Lent
Becomes more Lenten in this accident,
Henceforth your wavering flag no more hang out.

. . . .

If you will hang it out, let it weare
No more light colours but death's livery bear,
Hang all your house with black, the eaves it beares
With icicles of ever melting teares.[1]

There are some things that have escaped the theatrical antiquary, among them the fact that the custom of the flag long survived the platform-stage era. A flag is to be seen waving on the northern end of the Duke's Theatre in Dorset Garden in the interesting bird's-eye view of that notable house given in Lea and Glynn's undated Post-Restoration "map of London, Westminster and Southwark." [2] It was there in 1699 that Samson, the strong man of the period, gave occasional performances of his feats; and it was notified in the advertisements of

[1] Cf. the subtle reference in Jonson's epigram "To Mime" (no. cxxix) written before 1616:

"That still thou'rt made the supper's flag, the drum
The very call, to make all others come."

G. P. Baker, *The Development of Shakespeare as a Dramatist*, p. 51, in discussing the view of the first Globe in Hondius's *Map of London* (1610), says: "The flagpole rises from the centre of the enclosure, rather than, as in the later theatres, from a turret jutting inward from the tiled roof." But surely this was an impossibility.

[2] For an exemplar, see Gough Maps of London, vol. xxi, in the Bodleian. The view of the old Duke's Theatre referred to is reproduced (under a wrong attribution to Morden and Lea, 1682) in my article on the theatre in "The Architectural Review" for November, 1919, xlvi, 114.

the show that on the days of his performance a flag
would be hoisted on the theatre.[1] Truly, there was
wonderful vitality in these old Elizabethan customs.

Quite apart from the hoisting of flags and blowing
of trumpets, the garret (which, by the way, is to be
found clearly emerging from the building in the old
map-views of the Bankside theatres) had a variety
of other services. It was there the thunder was
made to roll, the lightning to flash, and the storm to
rumble. Jove's thunderbolt, otherwise a squib running slantingly on a taut wire, was launched thence
to kill the villain of the piece in the midst of his im-
precations on the lower stage. It was the Heaven
from which divinities descended in their "thrones"
to cut the Gordian knot which the dramatist had
so hopelessly entangled. Bells tolled there in
solemn moments, or (as in *Macbeth*) rang out in
wild alarm. Despite opposition to my old belief,
I am still of the opinion that it was in the garret
that those small pieces of ordnance known as chambers were let off so illusively in scenes of battle by
land and sea.[2] Professor Joseph Quincy Adams, a
formidable opponent, in disputing this view, points
out that we get directions for "chambers within"
but never for "chambers shot off above."[3] But I

[1] See the advertisement cited in Walter G. Bell's *Fleet Street in
Seven Centuries*, p. 336. When these lectures were first given at Harvard I was told by several of my pupils that the preliminary custom
of the flag was followed in the United States at football matches!

[2] *The Elizabethan Playhouse and Other Studies*, i, 9.

[3] *Journal of English and Germanic Philology*, xiii (1914), 358.

take leave to think that, unless we are expected to
assume that ordnance was never fired save from
stage level, this is a distinction without a difference.
The garret was a portion of the tiring-house, and
anything let off in the tiring-house was let off within.
There was danger attached even to mimic cannon-
ading, and the safest place for the firing of ordnance
was the garret. As it was, dire accidents happened.
The tamplin or stoppage of the chambers fired in
Henry VIII at the Globe lit on the thatch of the
surrounding galleries and, smouldering for long
unnoticed, started a fire which burned down the
theatre.

The helpful Elizabethan investigator is essentially a snapper-up of inconsidered trifles. The late
Thornton Shirley Graves was never happier than
when he lit upon a curious reference to the garret
in the "Character of a Player," written by one "R.
M." in 1629. It runs:

If his action prefigure passion, he raves, rages and protests
much by his painted heavens, and seems in the height of this
fit ready to pull Jove out of the garret where perchance he
lies leaning on his elbows, or is employed to make squibs
and crackers to grace the play.[1]

Remark here the mention of "painted heavens," a
phrase I shall have occasion to discuss later.

It has frequently been stated by competent

---

[1] Graves, *The Court and The London Theatres during the Reign of
Elizabeth* (Doctoral thesis, 1913), p. 25.

scholars that the garret occasionally served as a place of dramatic action.[1] We are told that scenes laid in towers or in other high places were generally acted there or thereabouts. At best, admitting the postulate for argument's sake, this could apply only to the public theatres; the private houses, though possessing a tiring-house, had no garret. The roofing of the entire building precluded its provision. We must bear in mind also that illusive pointing to the garret or tower by the players was one thing, and their actual use of the tower or garret as a place of dramatic action another. Of the illustrative use, there can be no doubt. Do we not find Juliet saying in the fourth act of the tragedy:

> O, bid me leap, rather than marry Paris,
> From off the battlements of yonder tower.

It is always "yon tower" or "yonder tower" that is spoken of in these cases.[2] But we cannot safely deduce from occasional reference to the tower by the characters that any of them ever resorted thither. In discussing matters of the Elizabethan stage it is dangerous to be literal-minded. It does not follow because scenes take place in a tower that

[1] Cf. Creizenach, *The English Drama in the Age of Shakespeare*, p. 377; R. Crompton Rhodes, *The Stagery of Shakespeare*, pp. 48, 49.

[2] See *Troilus and Cressida*, iv, 5, Ulysses' speech beginning, "Sir, I foretold you then what would ensue"; *The White Devil*, v, 1, "say, that a gentlewoman were taken out of her bed about midnight, and committed to Castle Angelo, *to the tower yonder*," etc.; *The Witch of Edmonton*, iv, 2, "would I had wings but to soar up yon tower."

they were necessarily acted in the theatre-tower. Such scenes are to be found in private-theatre plays, though the private theatre, as I have already pointed out, had nothing of the nature of a tower. Take Chapman's *The Gentleman Usher*, a Blackfriars play of *circa* 1606. Midway in the first scene of the fifth act comes the direction, "Enter Corteza and Margaret above." Margaret, in her distraction says: "I'll cast myself down headlong from this tower"; and, in a subsequent speech of Corteza's we read:

> Oh, 't is the easiest death that ever was;
> Look, niece, it is so far hence to the ground
> You should be quite dead long before you felt it.

If one did not know in what particular kind of theatre this play was acted, one would certainly be disposed to take the above references as proof that the tiring-house garret was occasionally used as a place of dramatic action. But public-theatre plays present evidence equally misleading, and not so readily confutable. Look, for example, at act III, scene 4, of *Lust's Dominion*, a play which has been assumed to be a revised version of *The Spanish Moor's Tragedy*, produced at the Rose early in 1600.[1] The scene is within a castle, and one notes the direction, "Zarack and Balthazar above with Calivers." Reference to their position is made in a speech:

> If Eleazer spend one drop of blood,
> On those high turret tops my slaves stand arm'd
> And shall confound your souls with murd'ring shot.

---

[1] Cf. H. Dugdale Sykes, *Sidelights on Elizabethan Drama*, p. 99.

Are we to take this literally? Is it to be supposed that most public theatres had two turret tops? Surely, the inference is that Zarack and Balthazar entered at either end of the first-story gallery. But it must be granted that in other cases the superficial implication is difficult to explain away. The task of reading the riddle set by act v, scene 2, of *Solyman and Perseda* is rendered all the more onerous by the fact that we do not know when or where it was acted.[1] Here we get a sequence of directions regarding the two witnesses, which, if designed for a theatre, would imply that the garret was really used as a place of action: "Then the Marshall beares them to the Tower Top . . . Then they are both tumbled downe."

Considerable as was the altitude of the tower or garret, it would not here have been a deterrent, since there can be no doubt that dummy bodies were used. It is notable also that in the conjuration scene (scene 4) in *The First Part of the Contention of York and Lancaster*, Elinor says, "and I will stand upon this Tower here," and that the direction which follows intimates that, "She goes up to the Tower." Later on, we have "Exit Elinor above." It was a considerable journey from the stage to the garret, and I see no reason in this case why it should have been undertaken. The gallery would have proved an equally satisfactory and much more accessible coign of vantage.

[1] Chambers, *The Eliz. Stage*, iv, 46.

There are, indeed, few more puzzling scenes in the old drama than these tower scenes. In this respect act v, scene 2, of Dekker's *Old Fortunatus* bears away the bell. After Montrose's order:

> Drag him to yonder tower, there shackle him
> And in a pair of stocks lock up his heels,

the ensuing action is difficult to visualize. We know that Ampedo and Andelocia are placed cheek by jowl in the stocks, but we do not know where the stocks are situated. If, on the strength of Montrose's order, one surmises that they are somewhere above, the chances are that one surmises wrongly. Ampedo dies and Andelocia is strangled in them. After the strangling, Montrose asks Longaville for a sight of the magic purse, and Longaville replies, "Here 't is, by this we 'll fill this tower with gold." But the subsequent action shows that the two are situated on the lower stage. They fight over the purse, and are interrupted by the entrance of a number of other characters through the two normal entering doors. Perhaps the right way to read Dekker's riddle would be to recall that his play bears signs of having been altered for court performance, and that in the process things got muddled.

As believers in the use of the garret or tower as a place of dramatic action Creizenach and Mr. Crompton Rhodes [1] pin their faith to the scene in the

---

[1] Creizenach, *The English Drama in the Age of Shakespeare;* Rhodes, *The Stagery of Shakespeare*, pp. 48, 49.

third act of *1 Henry VI* where is to be found the direction, "Enter Pucelle on the top, thrusting out a burning torch," assuming that "on the top" signifies a more elevated position than "above" or "aloft." [1] But does it? On this score, I content myself by again quoting one of William Archer's valuable unpublished notes:

It is very absurd to make the turret of the theatre the tower or turret from which Joan waves the torch. There were turrets on the walls of these French cities. At Orleans (see maps in Anatole France's *Jeanne D'Arc*), there were thirty turrets. Quite naturally therefore this tower would simply be a part of the wall, and no doubt the same part which had figured in 1, 4, as the turret on which Salisbury was killed. When the Bastard says, "the burning torch in yonder turret stands," fancy all the French leaders standing at the outer verge of the stage craning their necks to see past the edge of the "shadow" up to the turret of the theatre!

Archer's humorous reflection tempts me by natural transition to discuss the characteristics of the shadow or cover, whose main service was to afford the players a partial shelter from the elements and to protect their more or less costly hangings. In any consideration of the possibility of the garret being used as a place of dramatic action, the visual obstruction caused by the shadow, and affecting

[1] Brodmeier astonishes by assuming that "and Prospero on the top" in *The Tempest*, III, 3, 18, means that Prospero was hovering in the air. At first he almost decides upon the true reading, but eventually, because he thinks that the top machinery is required in the following scene (IV, 1, where Juno appears), he arrives at the conclusion that it was also used earlier. Which is a delightful *non sequitur*.

the dramatis personae and audience alike, must certainly not be overlooked. It affords, to my mind, an almost fatal objection to the theory. Let us look, for example, at the garret depicted in the Dutch sketch of the Swan. I am by no means disposed to maintain that it was of the common type, any more than I would be disposed to maintain that the theatre shown was of a standardized order, but it happens to be the only detailed view of a playhouse garret that has come down to us. Note that at one of the gables of the garret a trumpeter is to be seen emerging on a sort of narrow platform. In the Swan, this is the only possible place where top action could have taken place, yet — what with the obstruction of the shadow and the awkwardness of the position, situated as it was round a corner — very few people in the house could have seen what was passing there. Hence, I shall not, perhaps, be deemed rash for assuming that we have no solid evidence warranting belief in the employment of the garret as a place of dramatic action.

The shadow, cover, or heavens (all three contemporary convertible terms) was a thatched or tiled half-roof extending slantwise from the garret floor and covering at least one half of the stage. It had a gutterway to carry off the rain backwards, and it was generally supported by two massive pillars either resting on or going through the stage. Our chief authority for its characteristics is DeWitt's

sketch of the Swan, though it is disputed that
most of the shadows in the public theatres were of
the Swan type. When the Hope was built in 1613,
it was arranged that the house was to be used now
as a theatre and now as a bull-and-bear-baiting
arena, with a removable stage; and the building
contract specified that Katherens, the contractor,
should "builde the Heavens all over the saide stage,
to be borne or carried without any postes or supporters to be fixed or sett vpon the saide stage: And
all gutters of leade needfull for the carryage of all
such raine-water as shall fall uppon the same." [1]
The fact that the heavens at this house covered the
entire stage has induced several scholars to maintain that such was the arrangement adopted in all
houses built from 1598 onward. A quarter of a
century ago, M. Jusserand half assumed this attitude in expressing his belief that both the Globe
and the Fortune had a complete cover,[2] and at a
later period it was wholly adopted by Thornton
Shirley Graves and Joseph Quincy Adams. I post-
pone consideration of Graves's views for the moment. Adams has visualized his concept of the
typical or improved shadow in a conjectural design
of the Globe interior given in his valuable *Life of*

[1] Chambers, *The Eliz. Stage*, ii, 466.

[2] See his article on "Les Théâtres de Londres au Temps de Shakespeare," in *La Revue de Paris* for December 15, 1902, p. 722.

William Shakespeare.[1] His design shows a perfectly
flat shadow covering the great portion of the stage
and extending laterally from gallery to gallery, so
as to be self-supporting, the pillars beneath serving
as supports only for the projecting garret, which has
the shadow for its base. It is of a considerable ingenuity, and we have only to assume that the
scheme had been adopted at the first Globe to see
that the builder of the Hope would have no more
to do in obeying his instruction to eliminate the
pillars than to keep his garret flush with the tiring
house. But as Hollar's view of the Hope [2] affords
indication that he failed to take this course, the
postulate loses its cogency. Apart from that, however, there are two serious objections to Professor
Adams's scheme. In time of heavy rain, the level
shadow would have acted as a splashboard, adding
to the discomposure of the unprotected groundlings, and its full extent laterally would have mate-
rially darkened the rooms beneath, both in the
galleries and the tiring house.

It is notable that Mr. William Poel, who has done
so much good work in his day as a neo-Elizabethan
producer as well as by his vigorous propaganda,
is of the opinion that the shadow had its prototype

---

[1] P. 286. Adams's design is partly based on Graves's theory as
embodied in *The Court and the London Theatres during the Reign of
Elizabeth*, pp. 22–25, and in "Notes on Elizabethan Theatres," *Modern Philology*, xiii (1916), 113–116.

[2] Reproduced by Adams, *Shakespearean Playhouses*, p. 326.

in a similar device in the pageant car of the mysteries, which served the purpose of a sounding board,
such as we sometimes see over cathedral pulpits.[1]
Here we have one of those attractive, sensible,
tantalizing conjectures which scholarship, try as it
may, can neither confirm nor confute. It is by no
means with the desire of proffering an alternative
hypothesis that I take leave to point out that the
old Roman theatre in its latest period had a wooden
cover over the stage for the rejection of rain. Among
the theatres that we know to have been so equipped
were those of Orange and Aspendus. But the
ancient "shadow" was at too great an elevation to
give full protection to the players; and since it
tilted upward, it could hardly have been the prototype of the Elizabethan shadow. It is true that
the theatre of Orange was not seriously dismantled
before 1622, but it is doubtful if its Heavens, being
wooden and perishable, could have lasted anywhere
near that period.

As I am inclined to believe that the disposition
of the shadow as shown in the Dutch sketch of the
Swan was the normal disposition throughout, and
the complete cover of the Hope the exception, I
think it advisable to quote now from a letter on the
subject, written in 1907 by Mr. Walter H. Godfrey, the architect-antiquary, to the late William

[1] Article, "Concerning the Globe," in *The Stage* for October 7,
1909.

Archer, and placed at my services by Archer's executor. We three in those days were intensively studying the physical characteristics of the Elizabethan playhouse, and the main outcome of our deliberations was Mr. Godfrey's now well-known designs for a scientific reconstruction of the Fortune Theatre. Writing to Archer relative to the first draft of his Fortune plans, and replying to the suggestion that the shadow be made to cover the entire stage, Mr. Godfrey began by scouting the idea as improbable, and then went on to say:

I think, if anything, we have erred in making the "shadow" too large. If the stage is to project to the centre of the yard and all this is to be roofed, no builder would think of putting up separate supports for an independent roof. He would simply roof over half the theatre. In fact, such a roof would require the stronger support of the theatre walls. But since they did not roof half the theatre, it seems to me evident that the roof was there as an (unfortunately) necessary shelter at times, and would be made as small as possible. This is borne out by the Swan drawing, which (unless we reject it altogether) is surely valuable only in giving us just this little light on some of the arrangements. It would have been easy to draw the pillars in a different position had they been there. Besides which, the larger the roof is, the more light would have been excluded, and on dull days the stage and inner stage would be quite obscure.

I have already said that in early theatrical times, *shadow*, *cover*, and *Heavens* were all synonymous terms, but I purposely delayed pointing out that this, in part, has been disputed. Before entering, however, on this question, let us dismiss from our minds all thoughts of Professor Henry Thew Stevenson's wild theory that the shadow or cover was not a permanent half-roof, but a movable velarium, and this despite the fact that it has been echoed by so distinguished a scholar as Sir Arthur Quiller-Couch.[1] The identity of the three terms is by no means difficult to establish. What "shadow" indicates is best conveyed by an analogy drawn from contemporary female fashion. The shadow, or bonegrace, was a border attached to a bonnet to defend the complexion. It is not to be confused with the veil, which, however, was also worn. In the Fortune contract of 1599 we have mention of "a shadowe or cover over the saide stadge," apparently the same contrivance as "the heavens" of the Hope contract of 1613, which was to be built "all over the saide stage," and to lack posts or supporters. Years ago, I found substantiation of this synonymy in Heywood's *An Apology for Actors*, published in 1612, but evidently written a few years earlier.[2] In discussing the old Roman theatre, Heywood says, "The covering of the stage, which we call the heavens (where upon any occasion the gods descended) was geometrically supported by giant-like atlas." But for some years past, Professor Joseph Quincy Adams and I have vigorously disputed the

---

[1] Stevenson, *The Study of Shakespeare* (1915), p. 187; Quiller-Couch, *Shakespeare's Workmanship*, p. 45. See also, Lawrence, *The Elizabethan Playhouse*, ii, 6, 7.

[2] Cf. Chambers, *The Eliz. Stage*, iv, 250, introd.

point, both publicly and privately, he maintaining
that the heavens was the garret and I that it was
the shadow.[1] Honors now are easy, for as it happens, both were right and both were wrong. Neither
of us saw that the term was somewhat loosely applied. Higgins, in his *Nomenclator*, published in
1584, only a few years after the erection of the first
London theatres, defines "Machina" as "The
skies or coūterfeit heaven over the stage from
whence some god appeared or spoke." Here,
thoughts of the garret were evidently at the back
of the writer's mind. Similarly, Cotgrave, in his
French-English Dictionary of 1611, defines *volerie*
as "a place ouer the stage which we call the Heaven."
If *volerie* means "the flying place," otherwise, the
place from which divinities come, then the reference
must be wholly to the garret. Blareau tells us, in
discussing the staging of the old French mysteries,
that paradise was called, "a volerie," because it
was there the angels fluttered.[2] There is, moreover,
a passage in Hall's *Satires* (1597), dealing with the
players, which apparently equates the garret with
the Heavens:

> One higher pitch'd, doth set his soaring thought
> On crowned Kings, that fortune hath low brought.

---

[1] See *Journal of English and Germanic Philology*, xiii (1914), 357,
Adams's review of Lawrence's Second Series; also *Modern Language
Notes*, 1915, p. 70.

[2] L. Blareau, *Histoire de la création et du développement du drame
musical* (Bruxelles, 1921), p. 77.

Or some upreared high-aspiring swaine
As it might be, the Turkish Tamburlaine.
Then weeneth he his base drink-drowned spright
Rapt to the three-fold loft of heaven hight
When he conceives upon his fained stage
The stalking steps of his great personage.[1]

There was probably another reason besides its close association with the garret, why the shadow should have been sometimes spoken of as "the Heavens." It bore some resemblance to a canopy. Recall that Cotgrave, in defining *Dais*, writes of it as "a cloth of Estate, Canopie, or *Heaven*, that stands over the head of Prince's thrones; also the whole state, or seat of Estate." So, too, the tester of a bed was commonly known as "le ciel du lit." When the tester and a portion of his bedroom ceiling fell upon Charles Alexandre de Calonne, comptroller general of finance, in 1783, and nearly suffocated him, the verdict was "juste ciel!" Which reminds me that, because of the resemblance of the shadow to a canopy, Professor George Pierce Baker has seen fit to argue that the canopy referred to in certain stage directions in Marston's Blackfriars

[1] Cf. Prol. to *Henry V*:

> "O for a Muse of fire that would ascend
> The brightest heaven of invention,
> A Kingdom for a stage, princes to act
> And monarchs to behold the swelling scene!"

Also, The Valiant Welshman, 1, 1, opening, "Fortune descends downe from heaven to the stage, etc."

play, *The Wonder of Women*, or *Sophonisba* was in reality the shadow, and thence deduces a curtain hanging from its front.[1] How far he is astray in his reasoning will become apparent once it is grasped that the Blackfriars had no shadow. It would have been a superfluity in any enclosed theatre. Undoubtedly, in the private houses, the Heavens would be represented by the topmost story of the tiring-house.[2] In them there was neither garret nor shadow.

Recall for a moment R. M.'s significant reference in 1629 to the players' "painted Heavens." Deducing from this and other evidence, the late Thornton Shirley Graves, early in his lamentably brief career, formulated an ingenious theory to the effect that the inner side of the shadow was decorated with the signs of the Zodiac so as to symbolize the firmament.[3] He firmly believed that he had found a reference to this ornamentation in Aston Cokain's prefatory poem to Richard Brome's plays, published

---

[1] *Development of Shakespeare as a Dramatic Artist*, pp. 93, 94.

[2] Graves appositely quotes Formall's strictures on his rival from the third act of the Duke of Newcastle's *The Variety* (printed 1649):

"The Taverne he frequents he has made his Theater at his own charge to act intemperance; o'er the great Roome he uses to be drunk in, they say, he has built a heaven, a Players heaven, and thence a Throne's let down, in which, well heated, successively they are drawn up to the clouds to drink their Mistris health, etc., etc."

[3] Graves, *The Court and the London Theatres*, pp. 25, 26; *Studies in Philology*, xiii (1916), 113–115.

in 1653, in which, alluding to the Red Bull Theatre, Cokain writes:

> The Bull take courage from applauses given
> To eccho to the Taurus in the Heaven.

The only serious objection to this theory is that, assuming that it was vital for all sections of the audience to get a view of the signs, the signs could not have been painted inside a sloping shadow — unless, indeed, the slope was upward, as in the Latin theatre. To endorse Graves's view is to plump for a flat roof at a considerable elevation, and that is exactly what Adams does in his conjectural plan of the Globe already spoken of. Prior, however, to the publication of this plan, he had expressed his belief [1] that Shakespeare was making jocular allusion to the shadow when he wrote in *Hamlet*, II, 3: "This most excellent canopy, the air, look you, this brave o'er-hanging firmament, this majestical roof fretted with golden fire." With all due respect to a fine scholar, this is surely considering too curiously. The phrase "fretted with golden fire" hardly recalls a cover decorated with the signs of the Zodiac.

A good deal of false reasoning has been inspired by De Witt's sketch of the Swan. Although the contrary has been argued, it is certainly not drawn from any particular standpoint; but, if it could be

---

[1] See *Modern Language Notes*, xxx, 70.

taken as scientifically accurate, we should have to admit that the shadow not only covered a considerable portion of the stage, but extended round the two sides of the tiring-house. And as a corollary to this, we should also have to admit that the tiring-house jutted out beyond the circling boundaries of the galleries. But the truth is that De Witt (or Van Buchell, his copyist) first drew the right-hand extremity of the shadow as attached to the end of the base line of the garret; but, finding that this left the gable-end of the garret projecting awkwardly, and, recognizing that this, if unamended, would necessitate the shifting of the right-hand pillar somewhat to the left, he prolonged the shadow, to make it appear as if going round the corner, thus giving to the whole a highly misleading aspect. This side portion of the shadow, as represented, would have darkened the adjacent gallery without affording any compensating advantage.

In the course of a minute criticism of the Swan drawing published in *A Book of Homage to Shakespeare*,[1] Mr. J. Le Gay Brereton argues that the pillars are shown more widely apart than they were in actuality, and that consequently the garret was not so extensive as it appears. He also thinks that

it is likely that the upper stories of the tiring-house protected, so that the aerial descents could be made directly from the overhanging floor of the room above which the

---

[1] Pp. 204–206.

trumpeter stands, or even from the topmost chamber; it is significant in this connection that the front roof is not so extensive as the position of the pillars would lead us to expect.

There is good reason to take this as a satisfactory conclusion. I have examined a number of the exterior view of the Bankside theatres given on the old London maps, and I find that the garrets in all projected inward very considerably and were not flush with the outer theatre wall. They appear to emerge from the interior of the building. But the tiring-house itself must have extended to the outer theatre wall, since it was lighted (as the Fortune contract testifies) by outer windows. On the other hand, by admitting the inward projection of the garret, we can arrive at the conclusion that it was almost as commodious as any of the tiring-house stories.

The map-views of the old Bankside theatres deal with a variety of periods, covering indeed something like half a century; but it is noteworthy that only two of the views show turrets or minarets, the rest indicating garrets. The exceptions are (1) Visscher's view of the Globe,[1] which depicts a pointed square tower, with flag, standing between two hutch-like structures, the latter of which have been

[1] For a reproduction, see Adams, *Shakespearean Playhouses*, p. 253. The view is generally assumed to represent the second Globe, having been issued in 1616, but Adams maintains that the map was made from an earlier survey, and that the house depicted is Shakespeare's Globe.

conjectured by Mr. W. H. Godfrey to be staircase-
terminals; (2) Hollar's view of the Hope, issued in
1647,[1] showing a minaret arising between two large
twin roofs, a curious arrangement not to be justified
by any conceivable theatrical necessity. In one
sense, the Dutch sketch of the Swan corroborates
the evidence of the map-views. Its garret does not
reach to the outer wall of the theatre, nor does it
keep within the bounds of the topmost auditorium
circle. And it is, furthermore, of value in showing
two front windows and a gable door.

Though the Swan drawing affords us no evidence
on that score, it was apparently from the garret,
as Heavens, that divinities were lowered onto the
stage. Some consideration must now be given to the
modus operandi of these clumsy aerial flights. They
had been made from a fairly early period in the
history of the theatre. Traces of their occurrence
are to be found in sundry late-sixteenth-century
plays, such as *Sir Clyomon and Clamydes*, *A Look-
ing Glasse for London and England*, and *Alphonsus,
King of Arragon*, though in none of the three is any
mention made of the heavens. In the first, Provi-
dence simply "descends," in the second, Oseas the
prophet is "let down over the stage in a throne,"
and in the third, Venus is "let down from the top of
the stage." But it cannot be safely assumed from
the roundabout phrasing of the stage directions

[1] Reproduced by Adams, *ibid.*, p. 326.

that the term "heavens" was then unemployed.
Writing in his Diary, Henslowe, on June 4, 1595,
at a time some repairs were being done to the Rose,
records the payment of £7. 2. 0. "for carpenters work
and mackinge the throne in the hevens."

There can be little doubt that the pre-theatrical
inn-yard playing places had material influence on
the physical characteristics of the first theatres, and
in nothing more so perhaps than in the rude mechan-
ism provided for the flights of the gods. The old
carriers' yards were furnished with a crane and
windlass for the conveyance of goods onto waggons,
and there is reason to believe that the same principle was adopted in the early theatre garrets. Mr.
Walter H. Godfrey errs, in my opinion, in his well-
known Fortune plans, in suggesting the employment of a mere rope and pulley, but a good deal de-
pends, of course, on how far the god in his throne
was swung outward. I think, on the whole, that
Mr. A. Forestier, in making his individual plan for
the same house, was nearer the mark in indicating
the use of a windlass, for a windlass implies a crane.[1]
Here, unfortunately, the Swan drawing gives us no
help; for, so far from showing a crane, its garret
has no aperture out of which the throne could have
been swung.

To my mind the only real difficulty presented by

[1] Design published in *The Illustrated London News* for August 12,
1911, p. 276.

the problem of reconstruction is to determine exactly where the gods were let down. Clear space near the tiring-house was lacking; we have to reckon with the obstruction of the shadow. The throne could have swung clear of the shadow, if the shadow were short — say, much as it is shown in Albright's frontispiece — but in that case, the latter would have had no utility. Moreover, in reading in the old drama we occasionally come across situations calling for the use of the lowering apparatus in such a manner that the person drawn up or let down had to be close to the tiring-house. Take the basket-hoisting scene in *Englishmen for my Money, or a Woman will have her Will*, a Rose play of 1598.[1] Here, Vandalle was not only pulled up to upper-stage level but fairly close to the tiring-house front, because Alvario says to him, "A little farder, Signor Vandalle, and den may put you head into de window and cash he wensh." One recalls an analogous effect in the fourth act of *Antony and Cleopatra*. A great deal of pother has been made over the staging of the scene in which Antony is hauled up into the monument, but the solution is easy, provided we get the hang of things right at the outset. Diomed enters to Cleopatra from the back of the upper stage, and when she asks him if Antony is dead, replies:

---

[1] Act IV, scene 2, ll. 1650–1740; also ll. 2025–2072, in A. C. Baugh's redaction of the play (Philadelphia, 1917). The original is undivided.

His death 's upon him, but not dead.
Looke out o' th' other side of the monument,
His guard have brought him hither.

Then the guard, bearing Antony, come on below.
Bear in mind that, if Diomed entered from the back
of the upper stage, Cleopatra would face him as he
spoke, a position which would explain his reference
to the other side.   She was standing within the
room, not on the balcony.   Afterwards the dying
warrior is drawn up to the monument much as Vandalle's basket was drawn up, and by the same
apparatus.

Elaborating an idea of Albright's,[1] that man of
many talents who made so sad an end, the late Darrell Figgis, gives, in his *Shakespeare: A Study*,[2] a
neat design with the view of solving the problem of
the lowering.   He makes the garret jut out from the
tiring-house and project considerably over the
shadow, so that a throne lowered through a trap in
the garret floor might pass through a corresponding aperture in the shadow, and that without revealing the *modus operandi*.   This is feasible enough
in its way, particularly as there is sound reason to
believe that the garret did so project; but hard
fact has long ago lodged an objection to the theory.
We know from Ben Jonson's famous and much-
misinterpreted prologue to *Every Man in his
Humour* that the "creaking throne" came down "the

---

[1] Albright, *The Shaksperian Stage*, pp. 71, 72.   [2] P. 83.

boys to please," [1] that it was a thing delighted in of itself, apart from its utility as a dramatic expedient. Indeed, the machinery creaked to such an extent, and the throne was so long in reaching terra firma that, to suppress the grating sounds, it grew customary to play music or rattle thunder during the process. Thus, in the revised *Doctor Faustus*, as represented by the quarto of 1616, there is a scene toward the close where, as the hour of his doom draws near, a good and a bad angel come to visit the necromancer. When the good angel appears, we get the direction, "Music, while a throne descends." [2] After Jonson's sneer, it by no means surprises to find that rapidity of execution was far from being a characteristic of these aerial flights. In *The Prophetess*, ii, 3, Delphia and Drusilla appear above on a cloud drawn by dragons, and remain suspended in midair, listening unseen to all that is being said below. In a still later play, Rawlins's *The Rebellion*, iii, 2, there is a visualized dream in which Love descends

[1] See a similar reference in Lovelace's epilogue to the lost play, *The Scholar*, as published with his *Poems*. Albright, p. 73, gives a garbled quotation from this, and wholly misconceives its import. The gallery referred to was the auditorium gallery, not the gallery of the tiring-house.

[2] So, too, in *Cupid's Revenge*, a private-theatre play, Cupid makes several descents from and ascents to the heavens in the course of the action, and always to the music of cornets. Again, in *The Mad Lover*, v, 1, after loud thunder, and to the accompaniment of music, Venus comes down in her car.

halfway, but is arrested and sent back by Death's approach.[1]

Personally, I know of only one situation which lends any support to the Albright-Figgis theory. In *Cymbeline*, v, 4, we read that "Jupiter descends in thunder and lightning, sitting upon an eagle; hee throwes a thunderbolt. The Ghostes fall on their knees." Afterwards, at the cue "Mount, eagle to my palace crystalline," the bird ascends. Jupiter's flight is watched by the spirits, and at its finish comes the comment, "The marble Pavement closes, he is entered his radiant roofe." At a pinch, this might be taken as referring to Jupiter's disappearance through the aperture in the shadow. It is difficult, indeed, to see how we can avoid postulating that aperture. But, I believe that, if we could only determine what the word "firmament" signifies in a certain stage direction, we should have little difficulty in solving the whole problem. In Heywood's *The Brazen Age*, v, 3, we read that "From the heavens discends a hand in a cloud, that from the place where Hercules was burnt, brings up a starre, and fixeth it in the firmament." Hercules, after being struck with a thunderbolt, disappeared through a trap, and it was from the trap that the hand brought up the star. My own opinion is that here the word "firmament" signifies the shadow; but the point admits of no easy settlement.

[1] Note also the direction in *The Brazen Age*: "Medea with strange fiery-workes hangs above in the aire."

One other puzzle presented by front-stage "business" remains for consideration. I have purposely delayed broaching this matter because of its association with the shadow. Certain stage directions compel us to ask ourselves whether the pillars were ever pressed into dramatic service. Chambers thinks this highly probable,[1] and few investigators, I think, will disagree with him. But extreme caution must be exercised in assembling and reviewing the evidence. Occasionally, in the traffic of the Elizabethan scene we get mention of a post on the stage, but we must be careful to determine what kind of post is meant, since the stage had other posts besides the pillars of the heavens.[2] Moreover, we get references to posts in plays of the pre-theatrical period, such as *Jack Juggler*, *Gammer Gurton's Needle*, and *Cambises*.[3] Even in the face of this awkward circumstance, one would be disposed to say that all such references, say, after 1590, applied solely to the pillars of the heavens, were it not for the still more awkward circumstance that posts are occasionally pressed into dramatic service in seventeenth-century private plays, and this despite the fact that the private theatre, having no shadow, had no pillars. Take Day's *Humour out of Breath*,

[1] *The Eliz. Stage*, iii, 75, 76.
[2] Cf. the Fortune contract (Chambers, ii, 437): "saveinge only that all the princypall and maine postes of the saide frame and stadge *forwarde* shal be square and wroughte palasterwise, etc."
[3] Cf. Chambers, *ibid.*, iii, 37, 38.

a Whitefriars play of *circa* 1607. In act IV, scene 3, the boy fastens Florimel's glove to a post, and the blindfolded Hortensio takes it to be the fair lady's hand, and pays court accordingly. In this case, one of the balusters of the stage rails might have been utilized; but this reading cannot be applied to most of the situations in public-theatre plays in which posts figure. In Wilson's *The Three Lords and Three Ladies of London*, a Queen's Men's play published in 1590,[1] two posts are called for by the action in the last scene. Fraud is bound to a post and Simplicity blindfolded. Simplicity is to march and burn Fraud's face with a torch, but as soon as he is blindfolded, he is turned round thrice and left facing "the contrarie post," toward which he mistakenly goes. Here, surely, we have evidence of the existence of a supported shadow in some theatre in 1589, probably Burbage's primeval house. It is noteworthy that in two later plays, produced at different theatres, we get references to the employment of two associated posts. In *Englishmen for my Money*, line 1603,[2] Delio asks, "but watt be dis Post?" and Frisco not only tells him it is a maypole, but warns him of the presence of a second. In *The Atheist's Tragedie*, III, 1, there is a military funeral. D'Amville, referring to Montferres and

[1] Reprinted by J. P. Collier in *Five Old Plays*.

[2] In Baugh's reprint. Baugh sees in this a clear use of the pillars of the Heavens.

Charlemont, says, with appropriate action that can only be surmised: "There place their Armes, and here their Epitaphes"; and after he is obeyed, volleys are fired. After the second volley, D'Amville expatiates on the virtues of the father and son,

> So that on
> These two Herculean pillars where their arms
> Are plac'd there my be writ *non ultra*.

It is noteworthy that in that mysterious, belatedly printed play, *The Birth of Merlin*, there is a situation in which whimsical textual allusion was apparently made to the presence of the pillars of the Heavens. Act II, scene 1, passes in a forest. The Clown and his sister Joan are seeking for the father of Joan's unborn child. The Clown asks her whom he should inquire for, and she replies:

> Alas, I know not, he uses in these woods,
> And these are witnesses of his oathes and promise.

Here, she evidently refers to the pillars as trees, but the Clown, being by prescript a chartered libertine, chooses to take her literally, and rejoins with "we are like to have a hot suit on't when our best witness's but a Knight av th' Post."

There is also a number of old plays in which reference is made to the presence on the stage of a single post, and it may be useful to glance at a few of these references in something like chronological order. In Kyd's *The Spanish Tragedy*, III, 1, l. 48, we have the direction, "They bind him to the stake."

This looks like a simple utilization of one of the pillars. *Solyman and Perseda*, which dates from about 1592, is presumed also to have been Kyd's. In the last act of this play, the Marshal says to Erastus, "Thou shalt forthwith be bound unto that post, and strangled, as our Turkish order is." To most public-theatre dramatists of a later period, the temptation to press the pillars of the Heavens into stage service proved well-nigh irresistible. After all, it was more sensible to utilize a permanent post, when a post was required, than to place one on the stage for the purpose. It saved delay. In this Jonson was *à la mode*. In act III, scene 5, of the folio version of *Every Man in his Humour* we get the intimation, "Master Stephen is practising to the post"; and in the ensuing scene Cob says: "Then, I am a vagabond, and fitter for Bridewell then your worships' companie, if I saw any bodie to be kist, unless they would have kist the post, in the middle of the warehouse; for there I left them all at their tabacco, with a poxe." Nor is this all. In act IV, scene 7, a street scene, where Bobadil is holding forth on fencing tricks, we have the instruction, "He practises at a post."

At the dawn of the new century came Dekker's *Satiromastix*, first acted at the Globe and afterwards at Paul's. In the opening scene of the fifth act the dramatist availed of the post to spring a pun upon his audience:

> Daughter, stand thou heere, thou, Sonne Terrill, there.
> O thou standst well, thou lean'st against a poast
> (For thou 't be posted off I warrant thee:)
> The king will hang a horne about thy necke,
> And make a poast of thee.[1]

Of all puzzling situations in which posts play a part, none is more baffling than the one near the close of Greene's *Tu Quoque*, an early and very popular Red Bull play. A troop of friends conduct the Widow to her bedchamber in Sir Lionel Rash's house, and, after bidding her good-night, depart. Later on, she dismisses her maid, and then enters Spendall, who threatens her with a dagger unless she promises to love him. Policy induces her to feign consent, but we are sadly at a loss to know precisely what follows. The stage direction says, "Binde him to the Poaste." What post? a bedpost or one of the pillars of the Heavens? And how did she manage it unaided?

To practically the same period belongs *The Devil's Charter*, a highly sensational Globe play. In a scene apparently conceived as the bank of the Tiber, we find a bravo named Frescobaldi loitering around and waiting for some client who is to give him a certain watchword. Directions reveal that "the clocke strikes eleven" and that "he stands behind

---

[1] For other early examples, see Greene's *Friar Bacon and Friar Bungay*, scene 11, where Miles bruises his head against a suggested post; and *The Two Angry Women of Abington*, scene 11, where Coomes barks his shins in the dark.

the post." Undoubtedly, the only sort of post that would have answered here was one of the supporters of the Heavens.

Some curiously conflicting evidence is presented by two Red Bull plays between whose periods of production no more than a decade intervenes. First let us take Webster's *The White Devil*, which dates from about 1610. In its fifth act, according to the latter-day divisions, Gasparo, in dealing with Flaminio, says, "Bind him to the pillar" — an order which is at once obeyed. As there is no slightest hint of a pillar having been brought on, one naturally takes the reference to be to one of the pillars of the Heavens, and the conclusion may be right, notwithstanding that it is diametrically opposed to the evidence of *The Virgin Martyr*, a Red Bull play licensed in October 1620, entered on the Stationers' Register in December 1621, and published in 1622. In the fourth act of Massinger and Dekker's long-popular piece, we have the explicit direction: "Enter Dorothea led Prisoner, a guard attending, a hangman with cords in some ugly shape, sets up a Pillar in the middle of the stage, Sapritius and Theophilus sit, Angelo by her." Once they are seated, Sapritius says:

> According to our Roman customes, bind
> That Christian to a Pillar.

It is difficult to account for the discrepancy between the two plays. One could understand the necessity to set up a pillar in 1620, if by that period the Red Bull had ceased to require a shadow; and the curious thing is that we have some evidence that the house in its later days had been completely roofed, though the alteration can hardly have taken place at quite so early a period.[1]

Just one more illustration and I shall have done with this highly perplexing theme. Fletcher's *The Prophetess* was licensed on May 14, 1622, evidently for performance by the King's Men at the Globe. In act 1, scene 3, a street scene, when Geta is told that the dead boar has stirred again, he takes fright and hastily climbs up somewhere, much to the amusement of his companions. Maximinian, who is responsible for the hoax, says, "How nimbly the rogue runs up; he climbs like a squirrel!" and Diocles calls the panic-stricken one dunce, and bids him come down. Here again, resort to one of the pillars of the Heavens at once suggests itself, but, in our present state of knowledge, one can at best indulge in but idle speculation. Strive as we may, there are mysteries concerning the physical disposition and the customs of the old platform stage which obstinately refuse to yield their secrets.

[1] Cf. *The Fortnightly Review* for May 1916, p. 820, my article on "New Light on the Elizabethan Theatre"; Adams, *Shakespearean Playhouses*, p. 302 (where the date for the alteration of the Red Bull is approximated to 1625).